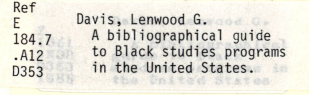

A Bibliographical Guide
to Black Studies Programs
in the United States

A Bibliographical Guide to Black Studies Programs in the United States

An Annotated Bibliography

Compiled by
LENWOOD G. DAVIS
and
GEORGE HILL

With the assistance of Janie Miller Harris

Foreword by Bonnie J. Gillespie

Bibliographies and Indexes in Afro-American and African Studies, Number 6

Greenwood Press
Westport, Connecticut • London, England

Library of Congress Cataloging-in-Publication Data

Davis, Lenwood G.
  A bibliographical guide to Black studies programs
in the United States.

  (Bibliographies and indexes in Afro-American and
African studies, ISSN 0742-6925 ; no. 6)
  Includes index.
  1. Afro-Americans—Study and teaching—Bibliography.
2. Afro-Americans—Bibliography. I. Hill, George H.
II. Harris. Janie Miller. III. Title. IV. Series.
Z1211.N4D38 1985 [E184.7] 016.973 '0496 85-12722
ISBN 0-313-23328-4 (lib. bdg. : alk. paper)

Library of Congress Catalog Card Number: 85-12722
ISBN: 0-313-23328-4
ISSN: 0742-6925

First published in 1985

Greenwood Press
A division of Congressional Information Service, Inc.
88 Post Road West, Westport, Connecticut 06881

Printed in the United States of America

∞

The paper used in this book complies with the
Permanent Paper Standard issued by the National
Information Standards Organization (Z39.48-1984).

10 9 8 7 6 5 4 3 2 1

For
James E. Newton
John Henrik Clarke
Percy E. Johnston

CONTENTS

FOREWORD

Professors Lenwood Davis and George Hill have compiled a most useful and valuable resource guide on Black studies programs that heretofore was not available. Such a basic compilation is a pathfinding effort.

Students, teachers, researchers, and bibliophiles of Black history will find this book a virtual gold mine of information, analyses, and critical evaluations of specific Black studies programs in the United States along with additional helpful related information.

But what is a Black studies program? How did the first one come about? Who started it? And even more preliminarily, why was there even a need for such a program in the first place? These and several other questions have been thoroughly attacked and answered in this volume, which speaks to its depth, perspective, and thoroughness.

Any serious student of American history knows that racism in America has impacted negatively upon all people, but especially upon Black people. And in the critical area of thought-transference via our written history, racism takes a Roman holiday. Thus, if we were to only go by what is written in our traditional textbooks, one would never know anything about the fact that Chrispus Attucks, the very first American revolutionary to die, was a Black man; that Harriet Tubman was a famous leader of the Underground Railroad who came to be known as "Black Moses"; that Nat Turner was a Black firebrand preacher who led one of the many famous slave rebellions; and that Frederick Douglass was an ex-slave who became a famous orator, abolitionist, Civil War recruiter of Black soldiers, public official, statesman, and diplomat. Such glaring omissions would lead one to believe that Black people contributed little to the construction, development, and maintenance of this western diaspora that we call the United States of America. So this book provides access to critical, missing information needed to "set the record straight," which is necessary not only for Blacks but also for whites who were the ones who confused and confounded the historical record in the first place.

Many of the inventions, notable accomplishments, and specific and general contributions by Blacks consistently over the years since Blacks have been on this continent have failed to surface in the standard, often read, history textbook written by the American historical establishment. Thus, had this flagrant sin of omission not occurred, there actually would be no need for Black history and/or any subsequent Black studies programs. But this would have been the ideal and it certainly did not happen.

What did happen was that the American historian (usually male) by and large being less than perfect wrote history that generally glorified his progenitors and himself. Thus, the contributions of anyone else—Hispanics, Asians, Native Americans, women, and Appalachian whites who were not white Anglo-Saxon Protestants—were selectively excluded from this "so called" American history. Thus, because of such obvious inaccuracies, oversights, and simple misrepresentations there arose a significant movement by revisionist historians. Black studies courses, programs, and the like appear to be a modern-day continuation of this revisionist reform movement.

Hill and Davis point out that although today's Black studies programs are most likely descendants of their 1960s progenitors, they still have a legacy that transcends the 1960s. They point out how Black historians like George Washington William, Edward A. Johnson, W.E.B. DuBois, and Arthur Schomburg wrote histories of Black Americans as far back as 1880.

Moreover, they note the seminal influence and contribution of Carter G. Woodson, a Harvard Ph.D. in history who founded the Association for the Study of Negro Life and History in 1915, *The Journal of Negro History* in 1916, Associated Publishers in 1921, "Negro History Week" in 1926, and *The Negro History Bulletin in 1937.* This one Black man almost single-handedly etched Black history into world history for all eternity to know.

Woodson was an indefatigable, devoted, and passionate advocate of "Negro History." His many works, including *Negro in our History, African Heroes and Heroines, History of the Negro Church,* and *The Mis-Education of the Negro*, are classics and should be required reading for anyone desiring to know anything about Black people in America.

Howard University, Fish University, Shaw University, Livingstone College, and Atlanta University—according to this book's authors—were the first higher educational institutions to offer and teach courses in Black history. And the fact that these events occurred as early as the 1920s in these historically Black institutions is no historical accident or coincidence. White colleges and universities were not even admitting Blacks let alone offering Black studies courses until the last quarter of a century by and large.

Even though such traditionally white colleges and universities as San Francisco State, Cornell, Columbia, Harvard, Berkeley, and Yale are those the authors found mentioned most often in the literature, these institutions were latecomers to acquire Black studies programs. Yet, these institutions apparently have the best such programs in this country. A question here is whatever happened to such programs in our historically Black institutions mentioned earlier? Are they alive and well?

This book annotates a series of accessible documents via its four chapters and culminating index. The first chapter consists of an introduction; the second chapter deals with general works and monographs; chapter three reviews some sixty-eight dissertations; and the last chapter analyzes and discusses over 500 articles and related works on this important subject. Newspapers are an important source of information on Blacks although they are not completely traceable. J. A. Rogers is one of the prolific writers on Blacks whose major contributions appeared within the Black press. One Black newspaper had a truism on its masthead: "We write about Black History Everyday." In my experience such a statement is rare given the racism, discrimination, and bigotry that exist throughout American institutions.

This book delicately and thoroughly deals with some of the past, current, and future critical issues of this fairly new discipline called Black studies.

Truly, Black studies programs make up a very young academic discipline in search of a paradigm. This, however, is no strike against it. These are the natural throes that a formal area of study must go through. This book, moreover, will make this search less muddled and cumbersome. This volume is one that is sorely needed today and hopefully will spawn others. It is a welcome addition to the growing stockpile of literature on Blacks and Black studies programs.

Bonnie J. Gillespie

INTRODUCTION

It would be nearly impossible to do an exhaustive study on Black studies programs because they are changing constantly. Therefore, this book can be neither comprehensive nor definitive. Moreover, much of the literature on the subject is written for limited distribution. Many Black studies departments only put out newsletters chronicling their individual achievements.

In this work we are not only concerned about the Black studies programs, departments, institutes, and centers, but the discipline as well. Although much has been written on the subject, to our knowledge there is no definitive bibliographical compilation. Many of the things written about Black studies are misnomers. There is a tendency to group almost everything written about the Black experience and Black culture under the title "Black Studies." The term Black studies used in this collection basically refers to the formal or structured discipline of Black studies in an academic setting.

Most individuals have the erroneous notion that the need for Black studies and Black history is a recent phenomenon. As early as 1880 Black historian, George Washington William, wrote *History of the Negro Race in America From 1619-1880. Negroes as Slaves, as Soldiers and as Citizens.* In this book Mr. William chronicled the history of the Black man in America from his earliest arrival to the Reconstruction era. About a decade later, in 1891, Edward A. Johnson, writing in *A School History of the Negro Race in America*, urges Black teachers to include the many brave deeds and noble characters of the Black race when they teach United States history. Professor Johnson also pointed out that the Negro is hardly given a passing notice in many of the histories taught in the schools.

Perhaps the earliest scientific historical book was written by William E. B. Du Bois in 1896. He wrote *The Suppression of the African Slave Trade, 1638-1870.* This monograph was Du Bois's doctoral dissertation written for Harvard University and was the first work published in the Harvard Historical Studies. Dr. Du Bois authored numerous other books, articles, pamphlets, and essays on Black history and the Black and African cultures, and did much to correct the many myths about the contributions Blacks made, not only to the United States, but to the world.

In the early 1900s, Arthur A. Schomburg, writing in *Racial Integrity: A Plea for the Establishment of a Chair of Negro History in Our Schools and Colleges*, advocated the establishment of courses in Black history in the public schools. He argued that no student was fully educated without knowing Black history and Black people's achievements. Mr. Schomburg believed that Blacks must write their own history.

A few years later, in 1915, Carter G. Woodson founded the Association For the Study of Negro Life and History. The following year he founded the *Journal of Negro History*. The journal soon established itself as one of the most scholarly and authoritative ones in the country. From its beginning the leading Black and white scholars published articles in it. Because it was so difficult to get publishers to publish books on Blacks, Dr. Woodson established a publishing company to publish books about Blacks. On May 29, 1921, he organized the Associated Publishers. Dr. John W. Davis was treasurer, and Louis Mehlinger served as secretary. Over the years, Associated Publishers published many books on Blacks. In 1937 Dr. Woodson established the *Negro History Bulletin*. This magazine had less scholarly articles than the *Journal* and contained pictures. The *Bulletin* was written for the public schools and young adults. He also started "Negro History Week" in 1926. Because of Carter G. Woodson's work in Black history, he is called "The Father of Black History."

Joel A. Rogers was another early Black pioneer in Black studies and Black history. For over fifty years Mr. Rogers devoted his life to researching and writing Black history. He was ahead of his times in many respects as it relates to Black history. It is only during recent times that researchers and writers validated positions argued by Rogers. He published his first book himself, *From Superman to Man*, in 1917, after it was rejected by several publishers. Rogers subsequently self-published several other books on Black history as well as several hundred articles on the subject in the Black press. Joel A. Rogers died in 1963 on the eve of Black students' protest for Black studies courses.

Over the years a number of Black journals were published that helped keep Carter G. Woodson's pioneering efforts alive. A partial list includes: *Opportunity* (1923), *Howard Review* (1923), *Journal of Negro Education* (1932), *Phylon* (1939), *Journal of Religious Thought* (1942), *Negro Educational Review* (1949), *Negro Digest* (1950), *Journal of Human Relations* (1952), *Journal of Social and Behavioral Sciences* (1954), *College Language Association Journal* (1956), *Negro Heritage* (1961), *Freedomways* (1961), *Dasein Quarterly Review* (1961), *Black Scholar* (1969), *Black Academy Review* (1969), *Afro-American Studies* (1970), *Negro American Literature* (1970), *Black Lines: A Journal of Black Studies* (1971), *Journal of Afro-*

American Issues (1971), *Northwest Journal of African and Black American Studies* (1972), *Journal of Black Psychology* (1974), *Pass: A Journal of The Black Experience and Pan-African Issues* (1975), *Western Journal of Black Studies* (1977), *First World* (1977), *Afro-Americans in New York Life and History* (1977), *Afro-American Journal of Philosophy* (1982), and *SAGE: The Scholarly Journal on Black Women* (1984).

Unfortunately, many of these journals are no longer being published. Percy E. Johnston, founder of the *Afro-American Journal of Philosophy*, is following in Dr. Woodson's footsteps and editing this journal on a full-time basis. Mr. Johnston stated the objective of the journal: ". . . we accept our obligations as participants in Afro-American tradition of philosophy journals. . . . *Afro-American Journal of Philosophy* serves its readers as a forum for discussion of important issues related to the advancement of human thought, including presentation of antithetical points of view. . . ." In the first issues of the *Journal*, Johnston discusses the historical media or journalism among Blacks beginning with Benjamin Bannaker's magazine in 1792.

Many people believe that since many white colleges and universities now have Black studies programs that Black history courses were first started there. The truth of the matter is that Black colleges taught Black history in the 1920s—if not earlier. Several of the private and church-related colleges taught Black history, such as Howard University, Livingstone College, Fisk University, Shaw University, and Atlanta University, to name a few schools. Moreover, southern Black segregated public schools taught some Black history or Black studies during the celebration of "Black (Negro) History Week" from the 1920s until the present. As a youth growing up in Beaufort, North Carolina, in the 1950s, I learned about great Black leaders and Black achievements. Blacks living in the North generally did not celebrate "Black (Negro) History Week" and, for the most part, knew little about the great deeds of Blacks. It would not be until the 1960s that the northern public schools began to teach Black history and the Black experience.

It was also in the 1960s that the modern-day Black studies movement got its impetus. It was the demands by Black students at white colleges and universities more than anything else that forced these institutions of higher learning to establish Black studies programs. Black students pointed out that Black people were not treated fairly in traditional textbooks and that most white professors made no effort to correct this omission. Therefore, Black students, along with the support of white students, demanded that specific courses on Black people and their history be taught as formal courses and taught by Black professors.

Carlene Young states the essence of Black studies in her essay in the 1984 Summer issue of the *Journal of Negro Education* (pp. 377-378) when she concludes:

The full responsibility for the development and implementation of appropriate, equitable, and just policies lies with the present generation of young adults, both black and white. Afro-Americans must ensure each new generation that existence of a sound knowledge base that informs and elucidates the history and experience of black people, and keeps them aware that their history is not yet an integral part of instructional materials and curricula offerings. This is the continuing role of Black Studies programs as they struggle to exist in an era of advanced technology, with rapidly changing social patterns and limited resources. The dream of Black Studies programs lies in the ability to provide the foundation which supports and enriches; to nourish the vision and motivation of present and future generations; and to reaffirm the continuity between past, present and future.

This Bibliographical guide deals with works by both Black and white writers. Chapter 1 includes seventy-nine major books and pamphlets on Black studies. The longest work in this section was edited by Gerald A. McWorter and consists of five volumes of the Proceedings of the Sixth Annual National Conference of the National Council of Black Studies.

Chapter 2 deals with general works and consists of seventy-two books. Many works in this section discuss Black students on white university campuses and their demands for Black studies courses. The schools most often discussed are San Francisco State, Cornell, Columbia, Harvard, Berkeley, and Yale. Little attention is given to the Black Studies Department at the Ohio State University. It is reported that this program is the "biggest" and "best" in the United States. This supposition is open for debate.

Chapter 3 consists of more than sixty-eight dissertations. The earliest was written in 1943 by Marie Elizabeth Carpenter. It is entitled "The Treatment of the Negro in American History School Textbooks: A Comparison of Changing Textbook Content, 1826 to 1939, With Developing Scholarship in the History of the Negro in the United States." Most dissertations that deal specifically with Black studies programs, however, were written in the early 1970s. The longest one was written in 1971 and contains more than 500 pages. The shortest one was written in 1972 and consisted on only eighty-five pages.

Chapter 4 includes more than 500 articles and makes up the largest part of this book. Major articles are denoted by an asterisk and include those articles that are usually ten pages or longer. Some shorter articles are listed as major if they take a different point of view on Black studies. An index listing authors, joint authors, and editors rounds out this resource guide.

We consulted all works that were available and attempted to give complete citation data. In a number of cases we saw only newspaper clippings of articles and not the complete newspapers. Many of the clippings did not give page numbers. Conversely, many of the papers are out of print and could not be located. We believe that this volume is the most complete reference guide of works by and about the subject to date. It is our hope that this work will help others better understand and appreciate the contributions that Black studies programs have made to American history.

We are indebted to Debra Stevenson and Margaret Nellon for helping with the proofreading and indexing. We would also like to thank Martha Rokahr for typing the final copy of the manuscript and for making several grammatical and technical corrections. Several libraries also assisted us: The Schomburg Center for Research in Black Culture; the Moorland-Spingarn Research Center; Wake Forest University Library; New York Public Library, Winston-Salem State University Library; and the Library of Congress.

Although many people assisted us in this endeavor, we take full responsibility for any errors or omissions and for all of its shortcomings.

A Bibliographical Guide
to Black Studies Programs
in the United States

1.
MAJOR BOOKS AND PAMPHLETS

1. A. Philip Randolph Educational Fund. Black Studies: Myths and Realities. New York: A. Philip Randolph Educational Fund, 1969. 45 pp.

   This is a collection of articles by both Black and White writers: Martin Kilson, C. Vann Woodward, Kenneth B. Clark, Thomas Sowell, Roy Wilkins, Andrew F. Brimmer, and Norman Hill. There is an Introduction by Bayard Rustin, Executive Director of the A. Philip Randolph Educational Fund. The authors discuss the negative and positive aspects of Black Studies. Most agree on the need for Black people to know their history. They disagree on the way to go about learning it....

2. Association For the Study of Negro Life and History. Negro History in The Home, School, and Community: A Handbook. Washington, D.C.: ASNLH, 1966. 47 pp.

   The material in this booklet is useful in class discussion, from the pulpit and the rostrum and in the communities. This study advocates the study of the Negro people in each unit of the courses in American History.

3. Ballard, Allen B. The Education of Black Folk: The Afro-American Struggle For Knowledge in White America. New York: Harper & Row, 1973, pp. 19-21, 25, 70, 72-74, 80, 104-118, 126, 143.

   Various references are made to Black Studies throughout this book. Chapter 6 is entitled "Blackening the Curriculum: White Universities and Black Studies." The author believes that the real end of Black Studies is not therapy but education to give young Black people a solidly grounded knowledge in things Black as well as a conceptual framework within whose contours they can begin to develop their own strategies for solving the problems of the Black urban

masses. The writer concludes that within the entire spectrum of
Black Studies programs one finds paradoxes; few Afro-Americans are
properly equipped to teach the courses....

4.   Banfield, Beryle. Black Focus on Multicultural Education: How to
Develop An Anti-Racist, Anti-Sexist Curriculum. New York: Edward
W. Blyden Press, 1979. 87 pp.

The material and procedures presented in this handbook have been
used with teachers and administrators and they have been developed
in accordance with several principles. The writer observes that materials dealing with the life, history and culture of Afro-Americans
should be integrated naturally into all areas of the curriculum.

5.   Banks, James A. Teaching The Black Experience: Methods and Materials. Belmont, CA: Lear Siegler, Inc./Fearon Publishers, 1970.
90 pp.

The essence of this book is that there is a need for Black History
for both Black and white children because both groups will have a
better understanding of themselves. Moreover, it was pointed out
that Black children that took Black courses had a positive effect
on the children's racial attitudes and self-concept. White children that used Black History textbooks resulted in marked positive
change in the subjects' attitudes toward Blacks.

6.   _____. et.al., Editors. Black Self-Concept: Implications for
Education and Social Science. New York: McGraw-Hill, 1972, pp. 7-
9, 22-23, 46-47, 49-52, 105-112, 141-143, 161-165, 171-172, 174,
195, 206.

The author points out that to help the Black child bolster his self-
concept, a number of school districts throughout the nation, responding largely to pressure from community groups, implemented
courses in Black History, hired more Black administrators and teachers, and purchased a flood of new textbooks and multimedia kits
which are sprinkled with "selected" Black heroes.

7.   Blackwell, James and Morris Janowitz, Editors. Black Sociologists:
Historical and Contemporary Perspectives. Chicago: University of
Chicago Press. 1974, pp. 253-266, 368-401.

Chapter 9 is by Nathan Hare and is entitled "The Contribution of
Black Sociologists to Black Studies." The authors state that Black
sociologists in general envision a "mutual" or "reciprocal" or "sym-
biotic" relationship between Black Studies and the Black community.
The Black Studies program would use people from the community as
teachers and paraprofessionals while the community would recognize
and utilize the competence and leadership of the Black Studies faculty toward community development and the elimination of social
problems. Chapter 14 is entitled "Response of Sociologists to
Black Studies" and is by Wilson Record. Dr. Record's essay was

based on interviews of 209 sociologists from 70 colleges and universities in the United States. Four basic patterns of response to the Black Studies movement occurred: embracement, antagonism, accommodation, and withdrawal or dropout. He concludes that young sociologists, Blacks and perhaps women were more favorably disposed toward Black Studies than might have been expected.

8.   Blake, Elias, Jr., and Henry Cobb. Black Studies: Issues in Their Institutional Survival. Washington, D.C.: Institute For Service to Education, 1976.

The authors suggest that Black Studies programs must have strong academic components if they are to be accepted at white institutions.

9.   Blassingame, John W., Editor. New Perspectives on Black Studies. Urbana: University of Illinois Press, 1971. 243 pp.

This work is a collection of essays on Black Studies. Most of these essays have appeared in other publications. The essays are: Nathan Hare's "What Should Be the Role of Afro-American Education in the Undergraduate Curriculum?"; "Ghetto and Gown: The Birth of Black Studies", by Roger A. Fischer; "Black Studies: Bring Back the Person", by June Jordan; Michele Russell penned "Erased, Debased, and Encased: The Dynamics of African Educational Colonization in America"; "The Case for Black Studies" was discussed by DeVere E. Pentony; Eldon L. Johnson dealt with "Race and Reform"; Jack J. Cardoso was concerned with "Ghetto Blacks and College Policy"; "Black Studies: Trouble Ahead", by Eugene D. Genovese; Kenneth B. Clark wrote "A Charade of Power: Black Students at White College"; "Black Studies at Antioch" was discussed by Stephen Lythcott; W. Arthur Lewis penned "The Road to the Top is Through Higher Education-Not Black Studies"; "Black Studies: An Intellectual Crisis" was written by John W. Blassingame; "Black Culture/White Teacher" was written by Catherine R. Stimpson; Darwin T. Turner dealt with "The Teaching of Afro-American Literature"; "Black History in the College Curriculum" was essayed by Joanna E. Schneider and Robert L. Zangrando; and "Black Studies and the Role of the Historian" by John W. Blassingame. There is also an appendix that includes "A Model Afro-American Studies Program: The Results of a Survey" by John W. Blassingame. A Selected Bibliography rounds out this book. Although there are disagreements among the contributors in this collection, many of them agree on several essential points: Black Studies is a legitimate and long overdue intellectual enterprise; it should and will produce changes in the attitudes of Blacks and whites; it will lead to improvements in the Black community and train more sophisticated leaders for it; and the program should stress scholarship and the solution of pressing social problems....

10. Bowles, Frank and Frank A. DeCosta. Between Two Worlds: A Profile of Negro Higher Education. New York: McGraw-Hill Book Co., 1971, pp. 108, 114, 124-127, 223, 248, 263, 275.

The authors discuss Black Studies at Merritt College, Miles College,

Morehouse College, and Morgan State College. The writers conclude: "But unless these efforts remain in the context of scholarship, orderly analysis, and the objective process of drawing conclusions based on facts, they (Black Studies) come to have no more meaning for truth and education than "agitprop" of Communist education, or the "Nazi science of Hitler."

11. Brisbane, Robert H. Black Activism: Racial Revolution in the United States, 1954-1970. Valley Forge, PA: Judson Press, 1974, pp. 5, 195, 223-244, 275, 292.

Chapter 10 is entitled "Black Studies". The writer asserts that a major focus of the Black Revolution after 1968 was the Black Studies Movement. Prof. Brisbane gives a brief survey of several Black Studies programs on white university campuses. He concludes: "By the fall of 1971 Black Studies departments and programs were no longer becoming political bases and cadre training grounds for Black Liberation.... Afro-American Studies on the high school, college, and university levels were steadily coming under the control of instructors and administrators, both Black and white, who were determined to establish the discipline as a standard facet of American education...."

12. Bryce-Laporte, Roy S. "Black Studies and the States: What Have They Done." Black Studies in Schools. Washington, D.C.: Education U.S.A. Special Report, National School Public Relations Association, 1970.

The title tells what this Special Report is about.

13. Butler, Johnnella E. Black Studies: Pedagogy and Revolution, A Study of Afro-American Studies and The Liberal Arts Tradition The Discipline of Afro-American Literature. Washington, D.C.: University Press of America, 1981. 154 pp.

This study provides cultural direction for the development of the field of Black Studies as it relates to Western curriculum and embodies human sensibilities. The writer concludes: "It holds strong implications for the process of education in this country and clarifies the concepts of Paulo Freire in his critique of Western education in the context of the American liberal arts tradition and the Afro-American reality." This is a revision of Dr. Butler's doctoral dissertation.

14. Carpenter, Marie Elizabeth. The Treatment of the Negro in American History School Textbooks: A Comparison of Changing Textbook Content. 1826 to 1939. With Developing Scholarship in the History of The Negro in the United States. Menasha, WI: George Banta Publishing Co., 1941. 137 pp.

This is a reprint of the author's doctoral dissertation that was written in 1941 for Columbia University.

15. Caselli, Ron. An Instructional Plan for Teaching Black History.
    Santa Rosa, CA.: Sonoma County Superintendent of Schools, 1970.

    The writer discusses the need for teaching Black History in the pub-
    lic schools in Santa Rosa, California. The author believes that all
    people should know the achievements of Blacks in the United States.

16. Cobb, Henry. Black Studies: Issues in Their Institutional Survival.
    Baton Rouge, LA: Southern University and A & M College, Unemploy-
    ment and Underemployment Institute, 1972? 50 pp.

    This booklet is a summary of a study of 29 colleges and universities
    that had Black Studies programs. This study discusses the following
    issues relating to Black Studies programs: 1. Structural Relation-
    ships to the Institution; 2. Theoretical Focus and Objectives; 3.
    Financing; 4. Staffing; 5. Enrollment Patterns; 6. Identification of
    Major Issues.

17. Cortada, Rafael L. Black Studies: An Urban and Comparative Curri-
    culum. Lexington, MA: Xerox College Publishing, 1974. 228 pp.

    The author probed the Black perspective of various disciplines, in-
    cluding the social and behavioral sciences, the humanities, and the
    natural sciences. He attempts to create awareness and sensitivity
    to the fact that there is no academic discipline that does not have
    its own special relevance to Black people, their needs, and their
    interests. This volume proposes general curriculum reforms in se-
    condary and undergraduate education, with Black and other minority
    studies as a basis. Prof. Cortada concludes: "The fact that aca-
    demic administrators have offered concessions rather than commit-
    ments must not be allowed to create a siege mentality among Black
    Studies scholars. They have a rare opportunity to develop a new
    interdisciplinary field that can be a liberating force for academic
    change and teacher growth, and that can restructure urban America's
    educational priorities for generations."

18. Daniel, Philip T.K. and Admash Zike. Black Studies Four Year Col-
    lege and University Survey. Dekalb, Il: National Council for
    Black Studies. 1983, 41 pp.

    The writers suggest that Black Studies faculty have produced almost
    3,000 publications, in the form of books, articles, papers, book re-
    views and others. They conclude that the most consistent theme that
    emerged throughout this study was the dual nature of Black studies:
    (1) Knowledge development or consciousness raising; (2) the psycho-
    logical independence of Black people.

19. Drewry, Henry N. Black Studies. Bermuda: The Bermuda Press, Limi-
    ted, For the Department of Education, 1970. 56 pp.

    This is an edited version of three lectures delivered by Professor
    Drewry to members of the teaching profession at Warwick Academy,

February 23rd-25th, 1970. One lecture was entitled "What is Black
Studies?" Lecture Two dealt with "Black Studies and The Curriculum".
The final lecture discusses "Black Studies: Materials and Techniques." Prof. Drewry concludes: "Black Studies in the curriculum of
our educational system is a necessary step but it is not the only
step. The full solution is a community wide matter in which all concerned must participate in seeking a solution."

20. Edwards, Harry. Black Students. New York: The Free Press, 1970,
    pp. 100-109, 205-227.

    Several Black students from San Jose State College, Columbia Univer-
    sity, UCLA, California State Polytechnical College, University of
    Texas, UCLB, Northwestern University, Indiana University, Luther
    College, University of Iowa and University of New Mexico give their
    feelings about Black Studies Programs curricula. An Appendix gives
    several Black Studies Programs curricula outlines from Federal City
    College, State University of New York at Albany and San Jose State
    College.

21. Evans, Charles J., Compiler. A Directory of Black Studies in the
    Chicago Metropolitan Area. Chicago: Innovation Center, Chicago
    City College, September, 1968. 11 pp.

    The compiler lists more than thirty colleges, universities, semina-
    ries, schools and organizations that offer courses in Black history
    and culture, including the Catholic Adult Education Center and the
    Central YMCA Community College.

22. Fisher, Walter. Ideas for Black Studies. Baltimore: Morgan State
    College Press, 1971. 51 pp.

    The writer gives a number of suggestions for teaching Black Studies.
    He points out that Black Studies courses can help students under-
    stand American History better, as well as themselves.

23. Ford, Nick Aaron. Black Studies: Threat-or-Challenge. Port Wash-
    ington, New York: Kennikat Press, 1973. 217 pp.

    This book, presented in layman's language is a professional evalua-
    tion of the past history, present practices, and future possibili-
    ties of Black Studies in the officially recognized educational pro-
    grams of American Colleges and universities. The author answered
    twelve significant questions on the basis of his personal interpre-
    tation of the facts: 1. What are the underlying facts concerning
    my involvement in this evaluative study of Black Studies in American
    higher education? 2. What is the origin of Black Studies? 3. Is
    the concept of Black Studies valid and viable? 4. What can a stu-
    dent do with a major in Black Studies? 5. Should all colleges and
    universities in the United States have organized programs in Black
    Studies? 6. What should be the objective of an acceptable Black
    Studies program? 7. What type of administrative organization is

best? 8. What kinds of courses should be offered? 9. What should
be a student's qualifications for admission to a Black Studies program? 10. What should be in the major qualifications for a director
of a Black Studies program? 11. Should Black Studies be organized
as a component of an Ethnic Studies program? 12. Are Black Studies
a threat or a challenge to American education? The author concludes,
in part: "Badly conceived and improperly administered Black Studies
are a threat to effective, meaningful, mind-stretching, truth-seeking
education. Badly conceived and improperly administered, and every
fair-minded observer must admit that such versions are definitely
in the minority...Likewise, thoughtfully and honestly conceived, and
effectively and wisely administered Black Studies are also a threat.
They are a threat to blatant ignorance of well-meaning people who
are supposed to know the truth about the entire history and culture
of their country and its people...." Black Studies are BOTH a
threat and a challenge, states Prof. Ford.

24. Foster, Julian and Durward Long, Editors. Protest: Student Acti-
     vism in America. New York: William Morrow, 1970, pp. 276-282, 406,
     416, 450, 459-482, 577.

     Various references are made to Black students and Black Studies pro-
     grams throughout this book. The writers point out that in most in-
     stances Black Studies courses were demanded by Black students at
     white universities: San Francisco, Berkeley, Northwestern, Cornell,
     Yale, Harvard, San Jose State....

25. Frye, Charles A. The Impact of Black Studies on The Curricula of
     Three Universities. Washington, D.C.: University Press of America,
     1976. 109 pp.

     According to Dr. Frye, the impact of the Black Studies Movement
     seems to have been more informal, more subtle in nature. There are
     four areas where this impact has been felt: 1. Student-faculty re-
     lationships. 2. Community involvement. 3. Recruitment methods.
     4. Confrontation politics. He states that Black Studies units
     which have already or will soon acquire departmental status will
     probably survive most of the vicissitudes which will befall the Am-
     erican university during the last two decades of the Twentieth Cen-
     tury. The author concludes: "In the main, Black Studies practi-
     tioners will successfully sidestep an issue which has been of cen-
     tral concern since the first Black Studies programs of academic ex-
     cellence."

26. _____. Toward A Philosophy of Black Studies. San Francisco,
     CA: R & E Research Associates, 1978. 86 pp.

     The philosophy of Black Studies discussed in this booklet explored
     some of the infinite possibilities of meaning contained in the va-
     rious levels of interpretation one may apply to the words Black
     and Studies. This philosophy suggests that the juxtaposition of
     these two words may be regarded as the ultimate creative equation,
     synonymous. Prof. Frye concludes: "Or stated another way, Black

is the essence of all things; Studies is the movement towards that
essence. All things are Mind; all 'movement' is mind in motion."

27. Giles, Raymond H., Jr. Black Studies Programs in Public Schools.
New York: Praeger Publishers, 1974. 157 pp.

The writer declares that the success of a district or school in developing a program in Black or Ethnic Studies will ultimately be determined by the ability of that school or district to organize a
program that makes it possible for individuals to realize their particular or diverse expectations within the same educational setting.
Dr. Giles concludes: "If there is anything to be concluded from the
findings of this study, it is that Black studies courses as presently developed in public schools can never be an effective or appropriate response to white racism, or a means of reducing prejudice
or discrimination based on white supremacist attitudes."

28. Goldstein, Rhoda L. The Status of Black Studies, Programs at American Colleges and Universities. Washington, D.C.: United States Department of Health, Education, and Welfare, 1972.

The author gives an overview of Black Studies programs. She discusses the failures and successes of Black Studies programs in selected
colleges and universities. A significant number of Black Studies
programs declined over the years.

29. Gordon, Jacob U. and James M. Rosser, Editors. The Black Studies
Debate. Lawrence, KN: University of Kansas, 1974. 160 pp.

This is a collection of essays that have appeared in previous pe-
riodicals that are listed in this book. The articles are: I. A.
Newby, "Historians and Negroes"; W. Arthur Lewis, "Black Power and
The American University"; Wilson Record, "White Sociologists and
Black Studies"; John W. Blassingame, "Black Studies: Intellectual
Crisis"; Robert L. Shelton, "The Meaning of Revolution in Black Revolution"; and June Albert, Rhoda L. Goldstein, and Thomas F. Slaugh-
ter, Jr., "The Status of Black Studies Programs at American Colleges
and Universities."

30. Gordon, Vivian Verdell, Editor. Lectures: Black Scholars on Black
Issues. Washington, D. C.: University Press of America, 1979,
pp. 1-45, 202-210, 291-293.

There are several essays in this collection that deal with Afro-
American Studies: Joseph E. Harris, "African History: A Prelude to
Black American Studies"; Harold Cruse, "The Academica Side of the
Movement and the Movement Side of Academica"; "Education in General
for Black People! For All People!", was written by Harry Edwards;
Roosevelt Johnson discusses "Afro-American Scholar: Issues and
Problems of Academic Publication Trends." There are two suggested
study Units and References for Introductory Afro-American and Afri-
can Studies: Unit One: Why Afro-American Studies: And Unit Two:
Africa, Africans and Afro-Americans.

31. Gunn, Evelyn, Editor. Black American Literature, Grades 10-12, Experimental. Cleveland, OH: Cleveland Public Schools, 1969.

The editor argues that Black American Literature should be taught in senior high schools.

32. Hare, Nathan. What Should Be the Role of Afro-American Education in the Undergraduate Curriculum? Washington, D.C.: Association of American Colleges, 1969.

The writer argues that the role of Black Studies should be to help bring about social change in society.

33. Harris, Janet. Students in Revolt. New York: McGraw-Hill Book Co., 1970, pp. 130-159, 143, 150.

Various references are made to Black Students demanding Black Studies programs at White universities: Columbia, San Francisco, Berkeley, Duke, City College of New York....

34. Harris, William H. and Darrell Millner, Editors. Perspectives on Black Studies. Washington, D.C.: University Press of America, 1977. 115 pp.

Chapter one deals with "Administration in Black Studies": Chapter two discusses "Role of Faculty"; Chapter Three answers the question "Is There a Need For Black History?" Chapter Four is concerned with "The Role of the Black College Student in the Development of the Black Community". Chapter Five deals with "The Research Role"; and Chapter Six discusses "Black Studies: A Projection". The goal of Black Studies is to bring into perspective the Black experience as part of the total human environment, state the editors. They conclude, in part: "Black Studies curriculum focuses attention on the problems of blacks in America and thereby indirectly on the problems of all non-dominate culture peoples - Black, Brown, Yellow, Red and White....While providing a sound educational offering to students, black and white, Black Studies is training technicians for work in the Black community.... "

35. Harvard University, Faculty of Arts and Sciences. Standing Committee to Develop the Afro-American Studies Department: A Progress Report. Harvard University, Cambridge, MA, September, 1969.

The title tells what this work is about.

36. Hoover, Dwight W. Understanding Negro History. Chicago: Quadrangle Books, 1968. 432 pp.

This book tries to provide a framework for the study of Negro History by presenting recent articles from historical journals and indicating some of the problems involved in reading and writing such history.

37. <u>Introduction To Afro-American Studies</u>. Chicago: Peoples College
Press, 1977. Vol. 1. 398 pp.

This textbook provides a systematic introduction to the historical
and current experiences of Black people in the United States. The
general aim of this book was to develop a standardized course, a
general introduction to the experiences of Black people in the United States, that can be used in Afro-American Studies Programs
throughout the United States and the world. This book has nine
chapters.

38. _____. Chicago: Peoples College Press, 1977, Vol. 2, 571 pp.

This is the first printing of the second volume of the Fourth Edi-
tion of this textbook. This books stands against all forms of exploitation and oppression, for freedom and liberation. This book
has 18 chapters, Sources of Readings and Appendix that discuss
"Why Should We Study Black People and How? Theory and Method in
Afro-American Studies."

39. Irwin, Leonard B., Compiler. <u>Black Studies: A Bibliography</u>.
Brooklawn, NJ: McKinley Publishing Co., 1973. 122 pp.

The title of the book is self-explanatory.

40. Jablonsky, Adelaide. <u>Media for Teaching Afro-American Studies</u>,
<u>IRCD Bulletin</u>. New York: Columbia University, Clearinghouse on
the Urban Disadvantaged, Vol. 6, Nos. 1 & 2, September 1970.

The author discusses the use of media in teaching Black Studies.

41. James, C.L.R., <u>Black Studies and The Contemporary Student</u>.
Detroit: Friends of Facing Reality Publication, 1970?, 35 pp.

The author argues that he does not believe that there is any such
thing as Black Studies. There are studies in which Black people and
Black history, so long neglected, can now get some of the attention
that they deserve, states James. He concludes, in part: "....I only
know the struggle of people against tyranny and oppression in a certain social and political setting and, particularly, during the last
200 years, it's impossible to me to separate Black studies from
white studies in any theoretical point of view...."

42. Johnson, Edward A. <u>A School History of The Negro Race in America</u>
<u>From 1619 to 1891</u>. New York: Isaac Goldmann Co., 1891. 200 pp.

The author urges Black teachers to include the many brave deeds and
noble characters of the Black race when they teach United States History. He points out that the Negro is hardly given a passing notice
in many of the histories taught in the schools....Prof. Johnson also
requested that his fellow teachers see to it that the word Negro be
written with a capital N. The writer concludes: "It (Negro) deserves
to be so enlarged, and will help, perhaps, to magnify the race it
stands for in the minds of those who see it."

43. Johnson, Roosevelt. Editor. Black Scholars on Higher Education in
the '70's. Columbus, OH: ECCA Publications, Inc., 1974, pp. 65-87,
89-111, 113-124.

Various references are made to Black Students and Black Studies
throughout this collection. Three essays are devoted specifically
to Black Studies: Nathan Hare, "The Battle For Black Studies". Dr.
Hare concludes: "Black students must help to structure a new ideology, provide models of revolutionary zeal for others, and activate
and energize the Black intelligentsia toward giving greater and
stronger direction to the people of the Black captive nation in
America...."; James A. Banks, "Teaching Black Studies For Social
Change." Prof. Banks concludes: "The goal of Black History should
be to help students to develop the ability to make reflective decisions so that they can resolve personal problems and through social
action, influence public policy and develop a sense of political
efficacy...."; and H. Oziri Ubamadu, "Developing a Relevant Afro-
American Studies Program." The writer concludes: "...a relevant
program should engage in actual problem-solving both on campus and
in the community...."

44. _____. Trends in Afro-American Studies: A Collection of Articles From The Journal of Afro-American Issues. Washington, D.C.:
ECCA Publications, 1975. 105 pp.

All of these articles appeared in previous issues of the Journal of
Afro-American Issues. They are: Nathan Hare, "The Battle for Black
Studies"; Nathan Wright, Jr., "Serving Black Students: For What?";
Gerald Eugene Thomas, "Resocialization of The Black Student Within a
New Permissive Education System?"; James A. Banks, "Teaching Black
Studies for Social Change"; Leroy Keith, "Issues Facing Black Stu-
dents and Faculty at Predominantly White Institutions"; William
David Smith, "Black Studies: Recommendations For Organization and
National Consideration"; Ewa U. Eko, "Consortium Approach To Deve-
loping African and Afro-American Studies: As Assessment."

45. Jones, Reginald L., Editor. Black Psychology. New York: Harper &
Row, Publishers, 1972, pp. 3-17, 136-165, 213-223, 252-272.

Several writers mention Black Students and Black Studies. One essay,
however, deals specifically with the topic: Cedric Clark, "Black
Studies or the Study of Black People?" Dr. Clark concludes: "While
it is true Black Studies has been late in beginning the scientific
advancement of Black people, we may note, in closing, that perhaps
it is better not to have advanced at all than to advance without
purpose or in directions where the correlation between psychological
knowledge and mental liberation have been all too low for Black people in particular, and the human race in general."

46. Kaiser, Ernest. In Defense Of The People's Black & White History
and Culture. New York: Freedomways, 1970. 64 pp.

The essence of this booklet is that there is a need for Blacks to
know their history and culture if they are to be liberated from racism.

47. Levey, Rose Marie Walker. <u>Black Studies in Schools: Review of Current Policies and Programs</u>. <u>Education U.S.A. Special Report</u>. Washington, D.C.: National School Public Relations Association, 1972. 50 pp.

This work discusses the pros and cons of Black Studies as well as case studies of various Black Studies programs all across the United States. Mrs. Levey concludes: "Black studies programs, although not without their difficulties, are already an accepted part of school curriculums...."

48. Lombardi, John and Edgar A. Quimby. <u>Black Studies As A Curriculum Catalyst</u>. Los Angeles: UCLA Students Store, May 1971.

The authors argue that students should take Black Studies courses in order to help bring about changes in society. They assert that Black oriented courses will help individuals to understand and appreciate the achievement of Blacks.

49. Long, Richard A. <u>Black Studies Year One</u>. Atlanta: Center for African and African-American Studies, Atlanta University, 1971.

The author gives a summary of the Black Studies program at Atlanta University.

50. Management Division of the Academy For Educational Development. <u>Black Studies: How It Works At Ten Universities</u>. New York: Academy For Educational Development, 1971.

The title tells what this work is about.

51. McEvoy, James and Abraham Miller, Editors. <u>Black Power and Student Rebellion</u>. Belmont, CA: Wadeworth Publishing Co., 1969, pp. 10, 120N, 169-171, 197, 207-212, 223-235, 291-292, 298-301, 440N.

Various references are made to Black Studies programs and Black students at selected colleges and universities, especially in the State of California. The essence of these essays is that colleges established Black Studies programs because Black and sometimes white students demanded them.

52. McWorter, Gerald A. Editor. <u>Philosophical Perspective in Black Studies</u>. Urbana, IL: Afro-American Studies and Research Programs, University of Illinois, 1982. 5 vols.

These are the proceedings of the 6th Annual National Conference by the Council of Black Studies. Vol. 1 dealt with "Race/Clan;" Vol. 2 is entitled "Studies on Black Children and Their Families"; Vol. 3 discusses "Philosophical Perspectives in Black Studies"; Vol. 4 is concerned with "Black Liberation Movement"; Vol. 5 relates to "Social Science and The Black Experience".

53. National Committee of Correspondence of the Pull The Cover Off Im-
perialism (PCOI). Introduction To Afro-American Studies: A Course
Outline-Guide For Study Groups. Nashville, TN: People College
Press, 1975. 55 pp.

The title tells what this work is about.

54. National Schools Public Relations Association. Black Studies in
Schools. Washington, D.C.: NSPRA, 1970.

This is a "Special Report" by the National Schools Public Relations
Association on Black Studies in schools.

55. Newton, James E. A Curriculum Evaluation of Black Studies in Relation to Student Knowledge of Afro-American History and Culture.
San Francisco, CA: P & B Research Associates, 1976. 102 pp.

This is a reprint of Dr. Newton's doctoral dissertation that was
written for Illinois State University in 1972.

56. New York (City) Board of Education. Black Studies: Related Learn-
ning Materials and Activities For Kindergarten, Grade 1 and Grade 2.
New York: Board of Education, Bureau of Curriculum Development,
1970, 227 pp.

The title tells what this work is about.

57. Nichols, David C. and Olive Mills, Editors. The Campus and The Racial Crisis. Washington, D.C.: American Council on Education,
1970, pp. 16-27, 62-63, 69-85, 86-95, 96-112, 235-240, 287-290.

Black Students and Black Studies are mentioned throughout this work.
One chapter, "The Validity and Utility of Black Studies," by Lawrence C. Howard is devoted specifically to Black Studies. The author concludes: "Black Studies is fundamentally a liberal art because its aim is to liberate mankind. Soul mixed with the Socratic
method will produce a higher education more devoted to man."

58. Orum, Anthony M. Black Students in Protest: A Study of the Origins
of the Black Student Movement. Washington, D.C.: American Sociological Association, 1972, 89 pp.

The author observes that Black students who are able to affect the
living conditions and curricula of colleges may give only the illusion of success. Whatever they do, the American educational system
is bound to change in the seventies because so many students are
realizing that it is not relevant to their needs and desires. The
development of courses in Afro-American studies will be only one of
many changes and it will undoubtedly come about, even without the
insistence of Black students, according to Orum. He concludes:
"We may have to wait many years to see whether the new programs of

Afro-American studies so arouse the consciousness of Black and white
youths as to produce fundamental changes in the American way of life.

59. Peterson, Marvin W., et al., Editors. Black Students on White Campuses: The Impact of Increased Black Enrollments. Ann Arbor, MI:
University of Michigan, Institute for Social Research, 1978, pp. 31-
37, 46-47, 81-82, 86-88, 90-91, 93-95, 98, 100, 104, 120, 131, 136-
137, 149, 164, 181-190, 191-193, 263-264, 301, 304, 307, 317-319.

The editors discuss Black Studies programs at the following colleges
and universities: Bradley University, California State College (PA),
Clarion State College, Lewis University, Macalester College, Northwestern University, State University of New York at Brockport, University of Missouri-Kansas City. It was surmised that the demand
for Black Studies courses was brought about by Black students.

60. Porter, Curtiss E., and Jack L. Daniel. Black Paper For Black
Studies. Pittsburgh: Black Action Society, 1969.

The authors state that Black Studies meant Black cultural history.
To them it also meant a relevant education that would give Black
students: 1. An accurate conceptual map of the world; 2. A knowledge of the conceptual maps and value systems of those who will be
affected by his activity; 3. An ability to see relationships and
alternatives that are invisible to most who have not had relevant
education; 4. An awareness of the importance of all areas of study
as opposed to study of one culture in isolation from the total body
of twentieth century, scientific knowledge....

61. Richards, Henry J. Topics in Afro-American Studies. Buffalo, NY:
Black Academy Press, Inc., 1971, pp. 1-7, 9-26.

Chapter 1 is by Henry J. Richards and is entitled, "Introduction:
Black Studies, The Liberal Arts and Academic Standards". The author
declares that thanks to Black Studies, the new liberal arts curricula are attempting to realize goals which heretofore were treated as
worthy but unattainable ideals. And, let us not forget the contribution of Black students and Black Studies to the elevation of academic standards, declares Dr. Richards. He concludes: "Black Studies as part of the liberal arts curriculum play a significant role
in developing in students an awareness of and respect for all cultural entities of the world as opposed to the almost exclusive concern with the ideas and ideals of Western Civilization which has
charaterized the traditional liberal arts curriculum....." Chapter
2 is by Donald Henderson and is entitled, "What Direction Black
Studies?" Dr. Henderson argues that the study of the Black experience will yield a proper perspective of the world Black experience
in historical and contemporary affairs of the world. Whites need
the knowledge of the Black experience to temper their unearned sense
of superiority. Moreover, such a contribution will place both the
Black and White experience in proper historical perspective and contribute to the correction of a good many historical untruths, states
the author. He concludes: "...Black studies...will truly constitute
..."education for Black power...."

62. Richardson, Irvine, Compiler. The Relationship of Africanist To
Afro-American Studies. East Lansing, MI: African Studies Center,
April 1969. 36 pp.

This is a report of a conference on the topic held at Michigan State
University, April 25 and 26, 1969. It was sponsored by the United
States Office of Education. The conference recommended that "each
university center of trained Africanists should seek to establish
appropriate relationships with the colleges and schools in its re-
gion so as to broaden the utilization of its competence at this special time, using local funding arrangements to the extent feasible."

63. Robinson, Armstead, et.al., Editors. Black Studies in the Universi-
sity: A Symposium. New Haven, CT: Yale University Press, 1969.
231 pp.

This book is the edited record of a symposium on Black Studies held
at Yale University in 1968. This was one of the first comprehensive
attempts to deal with the intellectual and political issues connec-
ted with implementing a program of Afro-American Studies. These papers constitute no definitive solution to the vast array of problems
pertaining to Afro-American studies, but they stand rather as an in-
dispensable pioneering inquiry into these questions. This book contains the following: "Preface" by Armstead Robinson; "An Introduction to the Conference" by Charles H. Taylor, Jr.; Harold Cruse discusses "The Integrationist Ethic As a Basis For Scholarly Endeavors";
"The Intellectual Validity of Studying the Black Experience" by
Martin Kilson, Jr.; Maulana Ron Karenga dealt with "The Black Community and the University: A Community Organizer's Perspective;
"Deck the Ivy Racist Halls: The Case of Black Studies"; by Gerald
A. Worter; Lawrence W. Chisolm did the "Summary and Commentary";
Donald H. Ogilvie gave "A Student's Reflections; "African History
and Western Civilization", was presented by Boniface Obichere;
Nathan Hare discusses "A Radical Perspective on Social Science Cur-
ricula"; "African Influence on the Art of the United States", was
written by Robert Farris Thompson; McGeorge Bundy discusses "Some
Thoughts on Afro-American Studies"; "On Teaching and Learning
Black History", by Edwin S. Redkey; Alvin Poussaint discusses "The
Role of Education in Providing a Basis For Honest Self-Identifica-
tion"; "Summary and Commentary" by Sidney W. Mintz; Armstead L.
Robinson wrote "A Concluding Statement"; David Brian Davis wrote
"Reflections"; An Appendix includes an Afro-American Studies Major
at Yale University. Dr. Robinson gives a summary of the concept of
Black Studies when he concludes: "American educators must face the
reality that their educational system has failed in the most fundamental ways to provide learning experiences that are relevant to
Blacks. They must also realize that the root cause of this failure
is racism - the type of racism, conscious and unconscious, which
dictates not only the choice of the materials to be presented and
the way they are presented, but also the way Black students' problems are perceived and dealt with by teachers and administrators....
The ferment among Black students is....about these fundamental problems and the urgent necessity for correcting them."

64. Rose, Alvin W. Afro-American Studies in Higher Education.
    Washington, DC: Center For Afro-American Studies, University of
    Miami, 1975. 42 pp.

    The author surmises: "...the issue of Black studies in higher edu-
    cation becomes vulgarized into the frighteningly polarized political
    question of whether retrospective forces can both cancel the small
    advance represented by existing Black Studies curricula and return
    to the parochialisms from which we all are trying to escape, or whe-
    ther the Black Studies curriculum can be strengthened to overcome-
    somehow and be immunized from its own plethora of inherent defici-
    encies...."

65. Schomburg, Arthur A. Racial Integrity: A Plea For the Establish-
    ment of A Chair of Negro History In Our Schools and Colleges.
    Yonkers, NY: Negro Society For Historical Research, 1913.

    In this Occasional Paper, No. 3, the author advocates the establish-
    ment of courses in Negro History in the public schools. He states
    that no student is fully educated without knowing Negro History and
    achievements. Mr. Schomburg believes that Blacks must write their
    own history. He concludes: "We (Negroes) must research diligently
    the annals of time and bring back from obscurity the dormant exam-
    ples of agriculture, industry and commerce, upon these arts and
    sciences and make common the battle ground of our (Negro) heritage."

66. Shagaloff, June. Survey of Negro History in Selected Secondary
    School System. New York: National Association For the Advancement
    of Colored People, Fall, 1969.

    This was an unpublished report of 212 school systems responses. It
    was found that the data indicated that for secondary school students,
    especially, a multi-racial, multi-ethnic, perspective for infusion
    into American history was preferred by secondary school personnel in
    urban, suburban and rural school systems.

67. Simmons, Henry F. Oral History and the Black Studies Program.
    Chicago: Chicago State College, 1968.

    The author surmises that oral history should be used in Black Stu-
    dies programs. Oral history is one of the few means that Black peo-
    ple used to preserve their history and culture.

68. Sims, William E. Black Studies: Pitfalls and Potential. Washing-
    ton, DC: University Press of America, 1978. 140 pp.

    The author suggests that one of the greatest pitfalls of Black Stu-
    dies programs is that they do not have the necessary support from
    white institutions. He also argues that Black Studies programs have
    the potential of changing society's attitude about the contributions
    Black people have made to American and World histories.

69. Smith, G. Kerry. The Troubled Campus. San Francisco: Jossey-Bass, Inc., 1970, pp. 42-43, 86, 149, 201-211, 212-219, 222-223, 245.

Chapter 21 was written by James Turner and is entitled "Black Studies: Challenge to Higher Education." He contends that Black Studies programs seek to remedy the total indifference of the American system of education to the needs of Black people. Chapter 22 is entitled "The Future of Black Studies" and was written by Vincent Harding. The author declares that the most difficult possibility that he sees for the future of Black Studies programs at White Campuses is the development of the programs into new campus forces. The force would need to be significant enough to transform the nature of the academic experience.

70. Smith, Joshua I., Editor. Library and Information Service For Special Groups. New York: Science Associates, 1974. 202-260.

Chapter 5 was written by Jessie Carney Smith and is entitled "Librarianship and Black Studies - A Natural Relationship." Dr. Smith declares that the natural relationship that exists between Black Studies and libraries is so pronounced that lines of separation of the two entities have virtually disappeared. She concludes: "In a sense, they created each other, and their natural dependency upon each other for survival is obvious. The library must continue to assume its role in providing adequate resources, facilities, services, and staff to meet the needs of Black studies and to ensure its future."

71. The State Education Department, Information Center on Education. Afro-American Studies in Colleges and Universities in New York State, 1968-69 and 1969-70. New York: University of the State of New York, 1970.

This work discusses the various Afro-American Studies programs in Colleges and Universities in the State of New York between 1968-1970.

72. Thorpe, Earl E. Black Historians: A Critique. New York: Morrow and Company, 1971, pp. 3-25.

Part One discusses "The Central Theme of Black History" and "The Why and What of Black History". Part Six discusses "Black History: Substance and Shadow". Dr. Thorpe surmises that Black History can be "pure" history, and as such is as justifiable as a separate entity as is state, regional, institutional, or national history. He concludes: "While Black history probably should not be a required course at any grade level, as an elective it should continue to have a place in curricula wherever and as long as there are interested and competent persons to teach it."

73. _____. The Uses of Black History. Raleigh, NC: North Carolina Department of Cultural Resources, Division of Archives and History, 1980. 14 pp.

This was a speech delivered during the observance of Black History
Week, February 11, 1980. The author declares that one very important use of Black history is to identify and define the Afro-
American people. Dr. Thorpe argues that the better this history is
developed, the easier it is for Afro-Americans to know with greater
completeness who they are, where they have been, and what they have
contributed in both positive and negative ways....

74. Valentine, Charles A. Black Studies and Anthropology: Scholarly
    and Political Interests in Afro-American Culture. Reading, MA:
    Addison-Wesley Publishing Co., 1972. 53 pp.

    The author argues that a reasonable and worthy task for anthropology
    and Black Studies working together might be to discover in full de-
    tail just how the Afro-American cultural and developmental processes
    work within changing socio-economic framework. Prof. Valentine con-
    cludes: "In other words, what is called for is a brand of scholar-
    ship which actively collaborates in efforts to change the existing
    social order radically, change it first of all in the interests of
    the people under study but no less in the interests of human beings
    in general...."

75. Walter, Mae. Editor. A History of Education of Afro-Americans in
    America. Millburn, NJ: RF Publishing, Inc., 1975, pp. 49-60, 197,
    237-252, 325-330.

    There are several essays that deal specifically with Black Studies:
    Lawrence Crouchett, "Early Black Studies Movements"; Janette Hoston
    Harris, "The Black Studies Crisis"; Barbara Lee Smith, and Anita L.
    Hughes, "Spillover: Effect of the Black Educated"; and Alvin F.
    Poussaint, "Education and Black Self-Image."

76. Walton, Sidney F. The Black Curriculum: Developing A Program in
    Afro-American Studies. East Palo Alto, CA: Black Liberation
    Publishing Co., 1969. 522 pp.

    This book redefines education for Black people into a day-to-day
    struggle. This work is also a collection of semi-official documents
    --memoranda, letters, reports, reprints of articles and studies.
    The author suggests that Black educators must become an advocate for
    the Black agenda; the white educators are also educated as to how to
    join the struggle to redefine himself. The writer concludes: "All
    Black educational environments...do not dehumanize Black children
    ...."

77. Wilcox, Preston. Black Studies As An Academic Discipline: Toward
    A Discipline. New York: Afram Associates, Inc., 1969. 16 pp.

    The author argues that Black Studies should not become perceived as
    being a reaction to the failure of institutions of higher education
    to include such programs as an integral part of their curricula. He
    states that Black Studies is an "academic discipline" fully accredi-
    ted within the Black world....

78. Wright, Nathan, Jr., Editor. <u>What Black Educators Are Saying</u>.
New York: Hawthorn Books, 1970, pp. 104-121, 126-182, 198-230.

Various essays in this collection discuss Black Studies: Benjamin
E. Mays, "Higher Education and the American Negro"; Nathan Wright,
Jr., "Can We Look At Harvard?"; Andrew Billingsley, "The Black Pre-
sence in American Higher Education"; Franklin H. Williams, "The
Black Crisis on Campus"; Edwina C. Johnson, "An Alternative to
Miseducation for Afro-American People"; Nathan Wright, Jr., "Black
Studies - Forecast From Hindsight"; John Henrik Clarke, "Black
Power and Black History".

79. Young, Carlene, Editor. "An Assessment of Black Studies Programs
in American Higher Education". <u>Journal of Negro Education Yearbook</u>,
Vol. 53, No. 3, Summer, 1984, pp. 199-378.

This entire volume is devoted to Black Studies Programs. The follow-
ing essays are included: Russell L. Adams, "Intellectual Questions
and Imperatives in the Development of Afro-American Studies"; St.
Clair Drake, "Black Studies and Global Perspectives; An Essay";
Locksley Edmondson, "Black American Educational Interests in the
Era of Globalism"; Guy Martin and Carlene Young, "The Paradox of
Separate and Unequal: African Studies and Afro-American Studies";
Alan K. Colon, "Critical Issues in Black Studies: A Selective Ana-
lysis"; Carlos A. Brossard, "Classifying Black Studies Programs";
James B. Stewart, "The Legacy of W.E.B. DuBois for Contemporary
Black Studies"; Denise M. Glover, "Academic Library Support for
Black Studies Programs: A Plea to Black Studies Faculty and Ad-
ministrators"; James N. Upton, "Applied Black Studies: Adult Edu-
cation in the Black Community - A Case Study"; J. Owens Smith,
"The Role of Black Studies Scholars in Helping Black Students Cope
with Standardized Tests"; Melvin K. Hendrix, John H. Bracey, John
A. Davis and Waddell M. Herron, "Computers and Black Studies: Toward the Cognitive Revolution"; Perry A. Hall, "Systematic and
Thematic Principles for Black Studies"; Delores P. Aldridge,
"Toward a New Role and Function of Black Studies in White and Historically Black Institutions"; and Carlene Young, "The Struggle and
Dreams of Black Studies". The goal of this work was to provide a
comprehensive yet invigorating overview of the discipline, suggest
new insights and directions, present examples of innovative approaches to the subject in both theoretical and applied terms, and
above all, to stress the importance of international perspectives
and linkages, especially with the African continent.

2.
GENERAL WORKS

80. Abrahams, Roger D. and John F. Szwed, Editors. Discovering Afro-
America. Leiden, The Netherlands: E. J. Brill, 1975, pp. 13-15.

    Chapter One is by Ulf Hannerz and is entitled "Research in the Black
    Ghetto: A Review of The Sixties". The author discusses the Black
    family within this essay and how its written history was changed
    over the years.

81. Altman, Robert A. and Patricia O. Snyder, Editors. The Minority
    Student on The Campus: Expectations and Possibilities. Berkeley:
    Center for Research and Development in Higher Education, University
    of California at Berkeley, 1970, pp. 179-188.

    Novel Smith wrote an essay in this collection entitled "Black Stu-
    dies". The author basically discusses the Black Studies program at
    Merritt College in California. He concludes: "...our black stu-
    dents have been saying to us, as they have been saying around the
    country, that in a truly multi-cultural society they shouldn't have
    to give up their cultural identity in order to be integrated into
    the majority culture. That is really what black studies is all
    about."

82. Arthur, Audrey C. "The Effect of Afro-American Studies on Atti-
    tudes of Black People." Black Life and Culture in the United
    States, Rhoda L. Goldstein, Editor. New York: Thomas Y. Crowell
    Co., 1971, pp. 341-346.

    The writer argues that Afro-American studies programs will provide
    the means to achieve equality; the natural drive and perseverance of
    the people, the will. Black people will begin to find ways of ex-
    pressing themselves within the framework of Black definitions, by
    Black standards, instead of according to what white society dic-
    tates.

83. Astin, Alexander W., et.al. The Power of Protest. San Francisco:
    Jossey-Bass Publishers, 1975, pp. 28, 78-80, 89, 91-94, 97-108,
    180-181.

    This work focuses on Black student protest for Black Studies at va-
    rious American universities. Most discussion, however, is devoted
    to Black students' demands for Black Studies at Columbia University,
    and Cornell University....

84. Bankston, Deborah. "Black Studies vs. Black Studies", Black Life
    and Culture in the United States, Rhoda L. Goldstein, Editor.
    New York: Thomas Y. Crowell Co., 1971, pp. 346-350.

    The writer contends that Blacks cannot let Black Studies in white
    universities placate them. She also suggests that since white uni-
    versities will only allow Black Studies to be taught from a white
    point of view, it is obvious that Blacks need AN ALTERNATIVE SYSTEM
    OF EDUCATION. This means that Black Studies in a Black Setting for
    the Benefit of the Black Community. The alternative for Blacks is
    to set up Black institutions which will perpetuate the system of
    BLACK NATIONALISM, not white racism. The purpose of the alternative
    system of education will be to establish a Black system in the minds
    of Black people..., concludes the author.

85. Becker, Howard, Editor. Campus Power Struggle. New York: Aldine
    Publishing Co., 1970. 236 pp.

    The essays in this book originally appeared in Trans-action Magazine.
    Various references are made to Black Students, Black Organizations
    and Black Studies at Berkeley, Columbia, Cornell and Illinois,
    throughout this collection.

86. Bell, Daniel, and Irving Kristal, Editors. Confrontation. New
    York: Basic Books, 1969, pp. 22-44.

    Chapter 2 is entitled "Black Studies at San Francisco State" and
    was written by John H. Bunzel. The writer not only discusses the
    origins of Black Studies at San Francisco State, but also at Yale
    University, Harvard University, Cornell University, and Stanford
    University. The author discusses Nathan Hare as the Coordinator of
    Black Studies at SFS. The Black Students at SFS made five demands
    to that institution that related specifically to Black Studies....

87. Blackwell, James E. Mainstreaming Outsiders: The Production of
    Black Professionals. Bayside, NY: General Hall, Inc., 1981, pp.
    20-24.

    It was stated that the students of 1968 and 1969 demanded courses in
    Afro-American Studies...on the predominantly white college campuses.
    Prof. Blackwell concludes: "In effect, not only did these students
    demand curriculum reforms, but significantly greater access to di-
    verse programs of study than those in which many Black students
    traditionally enrolled."

88. Boggs, James. Curriculum Studies For A Black Studies Institute.
New York: National Association For African-American Education,
February 12, 1969. 3 pp.

The title tells what this short leaflet is about.

89. Boyd, William M., II. Desegregating America's Colleges: A Nation-
wide Survey of Black Students, 1972-73. New York: Praeger Publishers, 1974, pp. 70-72.

It was pointed out that white colleges should include the study of
Blacks in their curriculums either through specific courses on the
topic or through revision of existing courses.

90. Brickman, William W. and Stanley Lehrer, Editors. Conflict and
Change On the Campus: The Response To Student Hyperactivism. New
York: School and Society Books, 1970, pp. 76, 88-90, 184, 457.

Some attention is devoted to Black students' demands for Black Studies at Columbia, San Francisco, Harvard Universities....It was
pointed out that Black campus leaders are extremely cautious about
forming alliances with white activists over campus's demands. They
avoid being used by the white activists for their (white's) own
ends, state the editors.

91. Bruce, Calvin E. and William R. Jones, Editors. Black Theology II:
Essays on The Formation and Outreach of Contemporary Black Theology.
Cranbury, NJ: Associated University Presses, Inc., 1978, pp. 53-77.

Chapter 2 is by Edward Leroy Long, Jr. and is entitled "Black Theology and Blacks on Campus". Prof. Long states that Black Studies,
once the preoccupation with winning the right to academic recognition is no longer needed, will be enriched only as criteria develop
for judging adequacy and competence. He continues to surmise that
the inappropriateness of traditional grounds for making judgments
about many aspects of Black Studies does not abrogate the fact that
such judgments will have to be made....

92. Chace, William M. and Peter Collier, Editors. Justice Denied: The
Black Man in White America. New York: Harcourt, Brace and World,
1970, pp. 538-548.

The last essay in this collection is by Michael Thelwell and is entitled, "Black Studies and White Universities". The author was
teaching Black literature at Cornell University during the Black
Student Revolt at that university. One of the demands that the
Black students had was for power and autonomy over their educational
life. Namely, they wanted Black Studies courses....

93. Coleman, James S. et al. Equality of Educational Opportunity.
Washington, DC: Office of Education, United States Department of
Health, Education and Welfare, 1969, pp. 273-275, 450-457.

This report states that the claim is made that the public schools,
whether integrated or segregated, are creatures of a white society
which does not recognize the ethnic needs of Black students. Teachers are charged with being "racist" in failing to understand
Black students and in using methods and standards which make it difficult for the students to find relevance in education. Curricula
have been modified to provide for the introduction of Black History,
suggest the authors.

94. Davis, Arthur, Jr., Racial Crisis in Public Education: A Quest For
    Social Order. New York: Vantage Press, 1975, pp. 75, 86, 117, 152,
    154, 155, 169, 172, 179, 214, 219, 227.

    The author asserts that the community wants schools with essential
    quality of providing an education that enhances the identity of
    Blacks, with Black Studies as an integral part of the curriculum.
    Davis argues that Afro-American culture does not presume to cover
    the full range of Black Studies, but is intended to be a coherent
    unit available to the community public schools as well as the insti-
    tutions of higher learning.

95. De Conde, Alexander, Editor. Student Activism. New York: Charles
    Scribner's Sons, 1971. 342 pp.

    Some attention is devoted to the demands made by Black students for
    Black Studies programs at Berkeley and Cornell Universities.

96. Divale, William Tulio with James Joseph. I Lived Inside the Campus
    Revolution. New York: Cowles Book Co., 1970, pp. 67, 70, 110, 182,
    207-212, 236.

    The writers discuss Black students and Black Studies throughout this
    work. They surmise that most Black Studies came about because of
    the demands by Black students at the following Universities: Cor-
    nell, Yale, Ohio State, Harvard, San Francisco....

97. Draper, Theodore. The Rediscovery of Black Nationalism. New York:
    Viking Press, 1970, pp. 148-167.

    Chapter 10 is entitled "Black Studies". The author traces the move-
    ment for Black Studies Programs from the earliest one, at San Fran-
    cisco State College, in 1966 through 1969. He suggests that Black
    Studies should be agents of social change.

98. Eichel, Lawrence E., et al. The Harvard Strike. Boston: Houghton
    Mifflin Co., 1970, pp. 62, 138, 205, 210, 238, 244-249, 254, 262,
    264-288, 311, 335-337, 346.

    The authors discuss the creation of an Afro-American Department at
    Harvard University. They point out that the Black students at that
    institution demanded that such a department be established at Harvard.

99. Epps, Edgar G. Black Students in White Schools. Worthington, OH: Charles A. Jones Publishing Co., 1972, pp. 84-101.

Chapter VI was written by Lamar P. Miller and is entitled "An Analysis of Objectives of Institutes and Departments of Afro-American Affairs." The author points out that the impetus for Black studies did not come from Black Students. The writer concludes: "The most fundamental question is whether or not Black studies can inevitably alter the character of the university in the decades ahead so that our learning experiences are not directed primarily at helping people learn how to make a living, but toward helping people learn how to live together."

100. Erlich, John and Susan Erlich, Editors. Student Power, Participation and Revolution. New York: Associated Press, 1970, pp. 94-117, 177-181.

Much discussion is devoted to the demands made by Black students for Black Studies at San Francisco State College, Columbia University, and University of Michigan. In most instances the Black students consider Black Studies to be an integral part of both the recruitment and the supportive services of those universities.

101. Fashing, Joseph and Steven E. Deutsch. Academics in Retreat: The Politics of Educational Innovation. Albuquerque: University of New Mexico Press, 1971, pp. 95-99, 191, 196, 199-200, 205-206, 229-232, 248, 252-253.

The author discusses Black Studies programs at San Francisco State, Berkeley, UCLA and Stanford University. Special attention is devoted to Black Studies at Stanford.

102. Foster, Julian and Durward Long, Editors. Student Activism in America. New York: William Morrow & Co., 1970, pp. 271-292, 319-344, 459-482.

Various references are made to Black Students and Black Studies throughout this collection. Three specific essays are devoted to Black Studies: Ralph M. Goldman, "San Francisco State: The Technology of Confrontation"; Lawrence B. deGraaf, "Howard: The Evolution of a Black Student Revolt"; Durward Long, "Black Protest."

103. Goldman, Peter. Report From Black America. New York: Simon and Schuster, 1970, pp. 143, 156-160.

The writer discusses the negative and positive aspects of Black Studies.

104. Gruabard, Stephen R. and Geno A. Ballotti, Editors. The Embattled University. New York: George Braziller, 1970, pp. 12-24, 60, 224-225.

105. Hale, Janice E. Black Children: Their Roots, Culture, and Learning Styles. Provo, Utah: Brigham Young University, 1982, pp. 10-11, 13, 155-156, 163, 175.

It was pointed out that Black Studies is a story of Struggle. Struggle is the key concept. The objective of Black Studies is to convey the struggle in which Black people have been engaged against European colonialism throughout history, across the African diaspora. A function of Black Studies is to enable each forms and disguises and to formulate a struggle against it, according to Dr. Hale.

106. Hall, Kenneth and Alfred Young, Editors. Education and The Black Experience. Palo Alto, CA: R & E Research Associates, Inc., Publishers, 1979, pp. 102-113.

Essay Eight in this collection was written by Harry Morgan and is entitled "Afro-American Studies: From An Idea to A Philosophy of Curriculum Building." The authors conclude, and rightfully so,: "In general Afro-American Studies must assume its role and position in the struggle alongside organizations, clubs, fraternities, and individuals who are engaged in the pursuit of total freedom and enlightenment for all non-White people of the world. We must do this in a spirit of trust and cooperation...."

107. Harding, Vincent. The Other American Revolution. Los Angeles: University of California, Center for Afro-American Studies, 1980, pp. 227-231.

Dr. Harding argues that it is true...that just as many of the energies of the middle-class Black freedom movement leadership have now been absorbed into the middle level structure of the American nation, so, too, the phenomenon that we called Black Studies - and many of its similarly middle-class proponents - has been absorbed into the structures, ethos, and aspirations of the American university system. He concludes: "...the Black Studies movement failed to carry to their logical, radical ends many of the challenges to the assumptions, ideology, and structures of American higher education, failed to continue to press the critical issue of the relationship between people inside the universities and those who will never make it...."

108. Harper, Frederick D. Black Students: White Campus. Washington, DC: APGA Press, 1975, 72 pp.

Part of Chapter 2 is devoted to a discussion of Black Studies. The author looks at the goals and functions of Black Studies. Many writers argue that one of the main goals of Black Studies is to correct American history by a more adequate recognition of the past and present experience of 25 million plus Black citizens..., suggests Harper.

109. Hercules, Frank. <u>American Society and Black Revolution</u>. New York: Harcourt Brace Jovanovich, 1972. pp. 417-424.

The writer argues that the need for Black Studies proceeds from the same order of urgency that dictated the student sit-ins in the South and other incidents of the general complex of Black protest and demand. Black Studies are invaluable sources, in their own terms, of the diversified cultural information necessary to the harmonious balance of a pluralistic society, states Mr. Hercules.

110. Hook, Sidney. <u>Academic Freedom and Academic Anarchy</u>. New York: Cowles Book Co., 1970, pp. 83, 92-93, 97-99, 101-103.

This work comments on the establishment of the Black Studies program at San Francisco State College. The program was headed by Nathan Hare. The author briefly mentions the formation of Black Studies at Harvard University. The writer questions the ways Black Studies programs came into existence.

111. Hurst, Charles G., Jr. <u>Passport To Freedom: Education, Humanism, & Malcolm X</u>. Hamden, CT: Linnett Books, 1972, pp. 159-175.

Chapter Seven is entitled "Black Studies". The author declares that the introduction of Black Studies as a legitimate part of the curriculum is one of the most refreshing educational developments of the 20th century. Dr. Hurst suggests that one ultimate aim of Black Studies programs must be the production of competent Black people in every scholastic and technical discipline to serve as teachers, community builders and leaders: He concludes: "<u>Drastic modification of credentialing practices may be the first major contribution of Black Studies to revitalizing of American education as a whole</u>."

112. <u>Index To Black History and Studies (Multimedia)</u>. Los Angeles, CA: National Information Center For Educational Media (NICEM), 1973. 189 pp.

This bibliography provides access to titles in seven media 16mm Films, 35mm Filmstrips, Overhead Transparencies, 8mm motion cartridges, audio-tapes, records, videotapes - filed under selected subject headings pertinent to the curriculum areas of Black History and Studies.

113. Jordan, June. <u>Civil Wars</u>. Boston: Beacon Press, 1981, pp. 45-55.

Chapter 6 is entitled "Black Studies: Bring Back the Person". The writer argues that Black American History prepares Black students to seize possibilities of power even while they tremble about purpose. According to Jordan, Black Studies helps Black people to know themselves; which they must do. She concludes: "...Black students, looking for the truth, demand teachers least likely to lie, least likely to perpetuate the traditions of lying: lies

that deface the father from the memory of the child. We request
Black teachers for Black studies. It is not that we believe only
Black people can understand the Black experience. It is, rather,
that we acknowledge the difference between reality and criticism
as the differences between the Host and the Parasite."

114. Ladd, Everett C., Jr., and Seymour Martin Lipset. The Divided Academy: Professors and Politics. New York: McGraw Hill Book Co.,
1975, pp. 4, 106, 129, 159-160, 206.

Various references are made throughout this book to Black Studies,
Black students, and Black faculty at white colleges and universities.

115. Lee, Don L. From Plan to Planet, Life Studies: The Need for Afri-
kan Munds and Institutions. Detroit: Broadside Press, 1973, pp.
55-61.

One section in this collection is entitled: "The New Pimps/or It's
Hip to Be Black: The Failure of Black Studies". The poet suggests:
"The formulation of black or Afrikan-American stidues at today's
white colleges and universities is only one of the super-mistakes
made in the Sixties. The future failure of Afrikan-American studies has been predicted and should not be seen as accidental by
any means...."

116. Liebert, Robert. Radical and Militant Youth: A Psychoanalytic
Inquiry. New York: Praeger Publishers, 1971, pp. 25-31, 45-47,
106-117, 164-165.

Various references are made to Black students and Black studies
throughout this work. Some attention is devoted to Black students'
demand for Black studies at Columbia University....

117. Lipset, Seymour Martin and David Riesman. Education and Politics
at Harvard. New York: McGraw-Hill Book Co., 1975, pp. 222-224,
340-342, 369-370.

The writers discuss the demands for an Afro-American Studies Department at Harvard university by the Black students on campus.

118. Low, W. Augustus and Virgil A. Clift, Editors. Encyclopedia of
Black America. New York: McGraw-Hill Book Co., 1981. pp. 270,
345-346.

The editors discuss the emergence of Black Studies and its curriculum. They state that Black Studies may be broadly defined as in-
tensive and scholarly studies of the Black experience in the United
States, including some related experience in Africe. The educators
conclude: "Whatever the approach, Black studies programs survived
the 1960's and early 1970's, but by the mid-1970's the elimination

or curtailment of these programs at some institutions because of low enrollments and lack of financial support caused some concern about the permanent survival of such programs in colleges and universities."

119. Major, Reginald. A Panther Is A Black Cat: A Study in Depth of the Black Panther Party-Its Origins, Its Goals, Its Struggle For Survival. New York: William Morrow & Co., 1971, pp. 68, 81-84, 131, 140, 154.

The writer points out that it was the demands of Black students on white college campuses that caused them to establish Black Studies Programs. He recalls the role that the Black Panther Party played in supporting Black Students in their quest for Black Studies Programs.

120. Malcolm X. Malcolm X On Afro-American History. New York: Merit Publishers, 1967. 74 pp.

Malcolm gives his views on Afro-American History. The leader discusses Negro History Week and points out this week reminds Black people only of the achievements they made in the Western hemisphere under the tutelage of the white man. Much of the information in this book was taken from Malcolm X Speaks.

121. Marable, Manning. From The Grassroots: Essays Toward Afro-American Liberation. Boston: South End Press, 1980. pp. 194-198.

One section is entitled "Black Studies and Black Struggles". The writer states that as Black Studies gradually emerged in the decade of the 1960's, it represented an expression of political dissent and cultural protest within the contextual framework of the white U.S. educational system. He said that the political meaning and content of Black Studies apart from its educational value, was the critical element of its development. Mr. Marable concludes: "Our struggle for Black Studies must become a transitional step toward our larger struggle to replace the entire educational framework of white Americans with a system of ethics and cultural values which will genuinely promote all the diversity and integral richness of humanity."

122. Mayhew, Lewis B. Legacy of the Seventies: Experiment, Economy, Equality and Expediency in American Higher Education. San Francisco: Jossey-Bass Publishers, 1977, pp. 59, 140-144.

It was pointed out that Black Studies was created to serve a multiplicity of purposes. Black Studies have been viewed as an important aid to develop a sense of Black identity and pride in students who were encountering for the first time the full impact of a predominant white culture. Secondly, Black Studies have been seen as a device to rectify deficiencies in curricula that had largely ignored the Black experience in the United States and Africa....

123. Meier, August, Editor. <u>The Transformation of Activism</u>. New York: Aldine Publishing Co., 1970, pp. 69-89.

William H. Friedland and Harry Edwards wrote an essay in this collection entitled "Confrontation at Cornell". They discussed the Black students' demands for a Black Studies Department at Cornell University.

124. Miles, Michael W. <u>The Radical Probe: The Logic of Student Rebellion</u>. New York: Atheneum, 1971, pp. 230-244.

The writer discusses Black students' demands for Black Studies programs at the following institutions: Duke University, University of North Carolina at Chapel Hill, Brandeis University, Cornell University, City College of the City University of New York, San Francisco State, San Fernando Valley State, San Jose State, and the College of San Mateo.

125. Moore, William Jr. and Lonnie H. Wagstaff. <u>Black Education in White Colleges</u>. San Francisco: Jossey-Bass Publishers, 1974, pp. 78, 108-113.

The writers suggest that community colleges have done more to include Black Studies in their curricula than four-year institutions have done, and in two-year institutions the administrator is more successful. The authors conclude that perhaps in no other area does the higher education establishment show its true conservative-if not racist-attitude is quite the same as the area of Black Studies....

126. Murray, Albert. <u>The Omni-Americans: New Perspectives on Black Experience and American Culture</u>. New York: Outerbridge and Dienstfrey, 1970, pp. 203-217.

There is one section entitled "Black Studies and The Aims of Education". The writer believes that a petition for courses in Black heritage is essentially only a request for a more comprehensive approach to the American heritage. He asserts that as long as Black students are allowed to ignore those fundamental intellectual disciplines and those broad sources of information that will enable them to question and evaluate the basic assumptions underlying all of the policies and programs being formulated for Black communities they are very likely to continue to entangle themselves in conflicting cliches....

127. Napper, George. <u>Blacker Than Thou: The Struggle for Campus Unity</u>. Grand Rapids, MI: William B. Eerdman Publishing Co., 1973, pp. 52-80.

This book examines the political world of the Black college student, especially those students at the University of California at Berkeley; and analyzes his registration of preferences in the milieu of

predominantly white institutions of higher learning. The author
discusses the politics that evolve as the Black Students at UCB
developed a proposal for a Black Studies Department.

128. Ornstein, Allan C. Race and Politics in School/Community Organiza-
     zations. Pacific Palisades, CA: Goodyear Publishing Corp., 1974,
     pp. 50, 154-157, 224.

     It was stated that there was a conflict over the direction and
     philosophy of Black Studies programs by Black militants and Black
     moderates. It was suggested that most Black Studies programs were
     usually propagandistic, anti-white, lacking in intellectual content
     and used by weak students to bolster their grade point average....

129. Phillips, Donald E. Student Protest, 1960-1969: An Analysis of
     The Issues and Speeches. Washington, DC: University Press of
     America, 1980, pp. 74-84.

     Various references are made throughout this book to Black students'
     demands for Black Studies programs at the following schools: Col-
     umbia, San Francisco, Cornell, Duke, Berkeley and Harvard.

130. Pinkney, Alphonso. Red, Black, and Green: Black Nationalism in
     the United States. Cambridge, England: Cambridge University Press,
     1976, pp. 178-204.

     The author observes that since the struggle for Afro-American Stu-
     dies commenced, schools throughout the country have been forced to
     introduce courses and departments in Asian, Chicano, Chinese, Jew-
     ish, Native American (Indian), Puerto Rican, and women's studies.
     It was stated that the first Afro-American studies program was es-
     tablished at San Francisco State College in 1967. It was also
     pointed out that in 1968 most of the colleges and universities
     agreed, as a result of pressure from Black students, to establish
     Afro-American Studies programs....

131. Predow, Karen. "Black Studies and Liberation, or Know the Real
     Enemy". Black Life and Culture in the United States. Rhoda L.
     Goldstein, Editor. New York: Thomas Y. Crowell Co., 1971, pp.
     350-359.

     It was pointed out that Black Studies must do more than survey
     Black history, drama, art and music; it must also...develop its
     world view and opinions in terms of the experiences of Black people.
     The author agrees that the task of Black Studies is to enable Black
     people to be able to start their analysis, organization, and fight
     for liberation from a base point that is clear in analyzing what
     has been done, and is being done, to Black people, states the
     writer.

132. Rist, Ray C. The Urban School: A Factory For Failure. Cambridge, MA: Massachusetts Institute of Technology Press, 1973, pp. 43-44.

The writer observes that teachers, and especially teachers of school-age Black children, should have competence in Black Studies, Black History, or Afro-American History. He concludes that the lack of training in Black Students has two serious consequences for the teacher in the Black classroom. First, without factual material, there is a randomness to discussions which offers students an incomplete view of Black people. Second, to give Black students a white history is to deprive Black students of their own history....

133. Romero, Patricia W., Editor. In Black America, 1968: The Year of Awakening. Washington, DC: United Publishing Corp., 1969, pp. 19, 62, 75, 90-93, 111-128.

Various references are made to Black Studies programs at a variety of colleges throughout the United States during 1968. It was stated that most of these Black Studies programs were established only after Black and some, white students demanded them.

134. Sampson, Edward E., and Harold A. Korn and Associates. Student Activism and Protest. San Francisco: Jossey-Bass, Inc., 1970, pp. 151-152, 193-195, 242-244.

It was stated that on college campus major Black students' demands have focused upon curricular changes: Black Studies colleges or departments established by Blacks, run by Blacks, teaching Black History, and the Black experience. The authors point out that Blacks often met great resistance for their demands for Black Studies departments set up by Blacks and administered autonomously by Blacks....

135. Schuchter, Arnold. Reparations: The Black Manifesto and Its Challenge To White America. Philadelphia: J. B. Lippincott Co., 1970. pp. 82-83, 88-89, 173-174.

The author suggests that Black Studies means the scholarly inquiry into the history of the Black man in America, a field which has been completely neglected and distorted at every level of education in the past. He concludes: "The psychological function of Black Studies programs, strengthening the black self-image and sense of blackness, underlies all of the functions of Black Studies."

136. Silberman, Charles E. Crisis in the Classroom. New York: Random House, Inc., 1970, pp. 96-100, 395-396.

Author suggests that public schools should teach Black Studies oriented courses along with traditional courses, if school is to be meaningful to Black students. He also points out that Black students' demands for specific courses and programs must not be ignored.

137. Smith, Robert, Richard Axen and DeVere Pentony. By Any Means Necessary: The Revolutionary Struggle at San Francisco State. San
Francisco: Jossey-Bass, 1970, pp. 6, 22-23, 30-39, 125, 132-136,
140-143, 147-157, 185, 207, 228-230, 320-325.

It was pointed out that at San Francisco State (SFS) a more militant, revolutionary conceptualization of the goals of Black Studies
emerged from the Blacks on campus. After the strike at SFS, Black
students and the Black community obtained a degree of influence
over curriculum, personnel, and administration never before granted
to students or the lay community. Dr. Nathan Hare was fired as
chairman of the Black Studies Department because of his leadership
role in demanding that SFS meet its obligations to Blacks on and
off campus....

138. Sowell, Thomas. Black Education: Myths and Tragedies. New York:
McKay, 1972, pp. 116, 178, 197, 201-206, 213-215, 261.

The author surmises that neither research nor teaching offers as
much opportunity for fulfillment to Black Studies faculty members
as to other faculty members. He states that Black Studies departments are, in effect, alienated from many of the leading scholars
in the field, and therefore alienated also from the major sources
of supply of future scholars with top-level training in the subject. Dr. Sowell concludes that for the foreseeable future, most
teachers in Black Studies departments will not be recognized as
scholars.

139. Staples, Robert. Introduction To Black Sociology. New York:
McGraw-Hill Book Co., 1976, pp. 298-300.

The author declares that the Black student movement did play an
important role during its heyday. It took many of the ideas of
Malcolm X, such as self-determination, the need to study Black
History and Culture, and the necessity to have education related
to the needs of the Black community, and raised them as issues.
Dr. Staples concludes: "By raising the issue of Black control of
Black Studies departments, they set good examples for the Black
community's quest for control of its schools, the police and other
institutions."

140. Strout, Cushing and David I. Grossvogel, Editors. Divided We
Stand: Reflections on the Crisis at Cornell. Garden City, NY:
Doubleday and Co., 1970, pp. 151-204.

Cleveland Donald, Jr. discusses Black students' demands for Black
Studies, Black Staff, and Black faculty at Cornell University between 1968-1969.

141. Taft, John. Mayday At Yale: A Case Study in Student Radicalism.
Boulder, CO: Westview Press, 1976, pp. 40-44, 82, 85-86, 112-115,
165, 170, 174.

The author discusses the role Black students and Black faculty
played in demanding that Yale University keep its commitmemt to the
Afro-American Studies program.

142. Thomas, Gail E., Editor. Black Students in Higher Education: Con-
     ditions and Experiences in the 1970's. Westport, CT: Greenwood
     Press, 1981. 405 pp.

     Various references are made to Black Students on white college cam-
     puses and Black Studies programs throughout this collection.

143. Thorpe, Earl E. Eros and Freedom in Southern Life and Thought.
     Durham, NC: Seeman Printery Press, 1967, pp. 166-174.

     Chapter VIII in this collection is entitled "Psychoanalysis and
     Negro Studies." The writer believes that psychoanalysis and Negro
     Studies are the far-reaching influence of psychoanalysis on twen-
     tieth century thought. This influence long has been evident in
     the novel, drama, and other areas, suggests Dr. Thorpe.

144. Tinker, Hugh. Race, Conflict and The International Order: From
     Empire To United Nations. New York: St. Martin's Press, 1977,
     pp. 87-88, 149.

     The writer points out Blacks not only pressed successfully for
     much larger admissions to colleges and universities, but they also
     demanded recognition of their own separate culture by programs of
     Black Studies....

145. Toole, K. Ross. The Time Has Come. New York: William Morrow and
     Co., 1971, pp. 9, 62, 109; 150, 166.

     The writer briefly mentions the Black Studies program at the Uni-
     versity of Montata (UM), Missoula, Montana. He states that Black
     students at UM demanded stronger and larger Black Studies programs
     at that institution.

146. Vargus, Ione Dugger. Revival of Ideology: The Afro-American
     Society Movement. San Francisco: R & E Research Associates, 1977.
     129 pp.

     Chapter 2 deals specifically with "Black Studies". This chapter
     points out that Black Studies must be in the vanguard of the pre-
     servation and development of Black values. Whether through the
     concept of "community" or "family", Black Studies must constantly
     reinforce the unifying tendencies which exist among Black people
     in order to guard against disintegration and extinction...Black
     Studies must clarify for Black people the myth that there are in-
     surmountable class distinctions between us which are basic to the
     problem of revolution....

147. Vermilye, Dyckman W., Editor. The Future in The Making: 1973
     Current Issues In Higher Education. San Francisco: Jossey-Bass
     Publishers, 1973.

     Chapter 14 is by Alison R. Bernstein and is called "Pluralism:
     Myths and Realities." The author discusses the origins of Black
     Studies at Vassar College. Vassar suffered its first sit-in by
     Black students in the Fall of 1969. The students' demands inclu-
     ded: the creation of a Black and Urban Studies Center, a chance
     for Black students to voluntarily live together on campus and the
     addition of Black faculty and Black Studies to counterbalance a
     lily-white faculty and curriculum. Eventually, the college ac-
     ceded to all of the demands.

148. Wilkman, Jon Kurt. Black Americans: From Colonial Days To The
     Present. New York: Universal Publishing and Distributing Corp.,
     1969, p. 55.

     It was stated that Black Americans have made many important musical
     contributions besides jazz and its influence. American concert mu-
     sic has been enriched by the careers of singers like Roland Hayes,
     Paul Robeson, Marian Anderson, William Warfield and others, de-
     clares Wilkman.

149. Williams, Bruce E. and Orlando L. Taylor, Editors. International
     Conference of Black Communication: A Bellagio Conference, August
     6-9, 1979. New York: The Rockefeller Foundation, June, 1980.

     Various references are made to Black Students and Black Studies
     throughout this book. One specific section is devoted to Black
     Studies and Black students: Melbourne S. Cummings and Jack L.
     Daniel, "Scholarly Literature on the Black Idiom."

150. Willie, Charles Vert. The Ivory and Ebony Towers: Race Relations
     and Higher Education. Lexington, MA: Lexington Books, 1981.
     pp. 115-120.

     Chapter 12 is entitled "Black Studies." The author states that
     Blacks insist on the immediate application of knowledge to the so-
     lution of community problems. They believe that a Black Studies
     program will accommodate this interest, that it will be less theo-
     retical and more pragmatic, and that it will deal with real and
     relevant issues. He concludes: "Black studies is a bona fide aca-
     demic program and deals with valid educational concerns. Black
     studies also is a political instrument through which power relation-
     ships between blacks and whites are balanced on white college cam-
     puses....Black studies is a manifestation of the movement for self-
     determination. Black studies is all of this - a complex and con-
     founding program."

151. Willie, Charles V. and Arline Sakuma McCord. Black Students in
     White Colleges. New York: Praeger Publishers, 1972, pp. 43-50.

Chapter 4 is entitled "Black Studies". The authors argue that
Black Studies is a bona fide academic program and deals with valid
educational concerns. Black Studies is also a political instrument
through which power relationships between Blacks and whites are ba-
lanced on white college campuses. They also point out that Black
Studies is a means for employment for Black professors at white
institutions. The writers conclude: "Black Studies is a manifes-
tation of the movement for self-determination. Black Studies is
all of this - a complex and confounding program."

152. Zimmerman, Matilde J. <u>Guide for Afro-American History</u>. Albany,
NY: New York State Department of Social Services, 1969.

This is basically a bibliographical guide to works by and about
Blacks.

3.
DISSERTATIONS

A SELECTED LIST

153. Abuso, Julian Elloso. "Symbols and Strategies in Black Studies: A
     Case Study." Unpublished Doctoral Dissertation, University of
     Pittsburgh, 1983. 238 pp.

     This case study of Black Studies Department (BSD) at Bridgetown Un-
     iversity (a pseudonym) examines the symbols articulated by two pro-
     fessors. It emphasizes the symbolic processes in ethnic conscious-
     ness raising and the struggle for academic legitimization. Symbolic
     actions observed through ethnographic participant-observation were
     the "non-political" causal dramas of the classroom, theatre, and
     other social action. The life histories of the two professors and
     a Black Studies major are also basic data for cultural analysis.
     Dr. Abuso concludes: "The two professors illuminate the interaction
     between ethnic and academic symbols. Interaction, which makes sym-
     bols powerful, resides in casual curricular activities, Black thea-
     tre, academic courses, and students' understanding of and expecta-
     tions from Black Studies."

154. Acholonu, Constance. "A Perceptual Analysis: Black Studies in Se-
     lected Community Colleges in Washington State, 1975." Unpublished
     Doctoral Dissertation, University of Washington, 1975. 213 pp.

     Dr. Acholonu surmises that Black Studies occupy a unique position
     in institutions of higher education. New concepts, new knowledge,
     new research, new technologies and new instructional methods have
     served to enroll new student populations and to facilitate new
     institutional and national goals. Little is known at present, how-
     ever, as to how Black Studies programs are actually perceived by
     various individuals both inside and outside institutions of higher
     education. She concludes: Students tend to think unfavorably to-
     ward Black Studies students and curriculum. Cause for concern cen-
     ters on the low regard of respondents towards the area of study and
     students. Black students have unfavorable perceptions toward Black
     Studies student majors and curriculum. Non-Black students had un-
     favorable to low perceptions of Black Studies majors and curriculum.

Exposure does not reduce unfavorable perceptions toward Black Studies students and curriculum. Students with no exposure have unfavorable perceptions towards Black Studies students and curriculum.

155. Addy, James. "Integration of Black History with United States History and Urban Geography with Modern Problems Courses in the Secondary Schools of the State of Maryland." Unpublished Doctoral Dissertation, George Washington University, 1974. 193 pp.

The purpose of this study was to examine the initiation of Black Studies programs into the 24 local school systems of Maryland and to determine the extent, the use, and the integration of Black History in United States history courses and of urban geography in modern problems courses in the course syllabi used in the secondary schools. Dr. Addy concludes: (1) The state has developed a K-12 multi-ethnic instructional program with a Black Studies component for classroom teachers and is developing a college-credit in-service Black Studies television program for teachers. (2) While all systems offered some form of Black Studies program, central office planning and program design varied widely or was non-existent among the 23 school systems. (3) The data indicated that few systems involved student or community representatives in planning and program design. (4) Implementation of Black Studies programs lacked coordination within school systems and among school systems in curriculum application, content, selection of materials, and in-service training for teachers. (5) Evaluation of Black Studies programs is excessively variant or non-existent among the 24 school systems. (6) While curriculum flexibility is desirable, many United States history and modern problems course syllabi vary in format, lack essential content, and are remiss in suggested teaching methodologies as those factors affect instruction about Blacks in America. (7) Most United States history and modern problems syllabi do not embody a multi-disciplinary format. (8) Urban geography as a discipline is not a part of most modern problems syllabi. (9) The Black experience in most United States history syllabi is not well represented according to present standards of historical scholarship. (10) Evaluation of course objectives through cognitive and affective instructional objectives is not well delineated in the United States history or modern problems syllabi.

156. Allen, Winston E. "Perceptions of the Real Role and the Ideal Role of Faculty Members in the Administrative Dimensions of Black Studies Programs in Undergraduate Colleges and Universities in the United States". Unpublished Doctoral Dissertation, Fordham University, 1972. 139 pp.

This study sought to determine and compare, by means of a four-dimensional faculty members' role perceptionnaire, the faculty members' perceptions of the real role and their role in the administrative dimensions of the Black Studies programs at undergraduate colleges and universities throughout the United States during the 1970-71 academic year. The investigation also attempted to ascertain the relationships between these perceptions of faculty members and two variables: (a) organizational structure; and (b) professional responsibilities in the Black Studies Program. Dr. Allen concludes: (1) The faculty members of Black Studies programs were not the primary decision-makers with respect to the administration of these programs. As a result, it would be seen that a valuable resource for administrative decision-making failed to be fully utilized. Of all the areas under investigation the faculty members had the least involvement in making the decisions with respect to matters related to the staffing of the program and with respect to all fiscal matters. There seemed to be a reluctance on the part of the college or university administrators to delegate authority to faculty members of Black Studies programs, especially in the areas of staffing and fiscal matters, without any clearly discernable reason. (2) The areas of planning and evaluating were selected by faculty members as those in which they had the greatest opportunity to participate in the decision-making process. In addition, these two areas were the ones in which the faculty members indicated that they wished to be most active in the decision-making process. Apparently, this resulted from the fact that of all the areas studied, the areas of planning and evaluating were the ones in which the faculty members had the greatest expertise. (3) There was a true difference between the actual and the preferred roles of Black Studies faculty members in almost every instance, with the faculty members desiring more decision-making power than they actually had. This seemed to support the view that the faculty members of Black Studies programs constituted a highly motivated and committed component in the program and as such this group should have been used to a much greater extent in the administrative decision-making process of the programs in order to further the goals of these programs....

157. Andrews, Pearl T. "A Study of the Effects of 'Black Studies' on the Self-Concept of Negro Kindergarten Children." Unpublished Doctoral Dissertation, University of Illinois at Urbana-Champaign, 1971. 154 pp.

The purpose of this study was to examine the effects of Black Studies on the self-concept of Negro five-year-old preschool children, and the relationship of this self-concept to their school achievement. Black Studies was defined as a systematic program of study about past and present Negro contributions to American culture. The results tended to support the four basic research questions posited for the study: (1) A Black Studies program for kindergarten children proved effective, as shown by the children's responses to items on the knowledge test. (2) Negro children developed a more positive self-concept as a result of being exposed to the program. (3) Negro children improved in readiness test scores, and (4) There was a low but positive relationship between achievement gain and self-concept increase. It was thus concluded that school as a social institution, and the content of the curriculum, are two essential aspects of a child's learning experience which can significantly influence the Black child's self-concept and readiness for school achievement. The findings of this study further supported the strategic importance and value of introducing children to an accurate and fair view of the contributions of all racial groups. It was concluded that if one can positively affect the self-concept of young Black children, by showing them the major contributions of their race, one may also aid in erasing much of the early-school difficulties teachers have experienced in reaching minority group children.

158. Arnold, Margaret L. "A Plan For Incorporating Black Studies Into The General Education Program of a Community College." Unpublished Doctoral Dissertation, University of Florida, 1973. 175 pp.

This study proposed to develop a plan, within a humanistic framework, by which Black Studies material could be incorporated into the general education curriculum of a selected community college. The plan included four basic elements: (1) A rationale for inclusion of Black Studies material into the general education program of a community college. (2) The basic objectives that were to be reached by including the material in the program. (3) The learning activities through which these objectives could be reached. (4) Evaluation procedures for determining the effectiveness with which the objectives were met. The primary aim in developing this plan was to provide material - objectives, learning activities, and methods of evaluation - which could be used in a selected community college. Also, since accurate material about Black people is not widely known, this study may serve as teacher resource material for those instructors who are not knowledgeable about Black people, their history, and their accomplishments. The data presented here are not universal. Rather, they are only examples of suggested methods and materials which can be used in similar programs of other community colleges. What is needed is further research to determine the extent to which such added material as is presented in this study would change the concepts Blacks have about themselves and of other groups about Black people, argues Dr. Arnold.

159. Bailey, Ronald William. "The Slave Trade and The Development of Capitalism in the United States: A Critical Reappraisal of Theory and Method in Afro-American Studies." Unpublished Doctoral Dissertation, Stanford University, 1980. 358 pp.

The central thesis of this dissertation is that the involvement in the slave trade and related economic activity by New England merchants made a large and essential contribution to the colonial phase of the development of U.S. capitalism and imperialism. Using the theory of Marxist political economy, it argues that it is incorrect to isolate the slave trade as the sale of bodies and then to conclude, as several recent studies have done, that the slave trade was not "a" or "the" decisive component in capitalist development. Rather, the slave trade and the economic activity related to it (e.g., rum manufacturing) must be viewed as integral components of a process which led to two developments. The dissertation also explores the recent decade of the rise of Black Studies as a discipline of study, the intellectual context of this study. A key aspect of this period and a tradition in the history of Black scholars has been a commitment to the struggle for academic excellence and social responsibility, to contribute to a politically relevant scholarship which serves the struggle for Black liberation and social change, concludes Dr. Bailey.

160. Bartley, Melinda. "A Study of the Effects of Career Orientation on The Level of Job Satisfaction of Directors of Black Studies Program." Unpublished Doctoral Dissertation, George Washington University, 1977. 114 pp.

The purpose of the study was to determine the effects of career orientation on the levels of job satisfaction of directors of Black Studies Programs. The study also sought to determine whether relationships exist between occupational and educational expectations and aspirations of directors of Black Studies Programs. Job satisfaction was conceptualized as a multidimensional concept involving reward satisfaction, intrinsic satisfaction and concomitant satisfaction. Career orientation was conceptualized as consisting of both the aspirations and the expectations concerning educational and occupational achievements. Job satisfaction was the dependent variable in the study, while career orientation was the independent variable. The sample for the study consisted of 102 directors of Black Studies Programs selected at colleges and universities from the four geographic regions of the United States. The writer concludes: (1) Directors of Black Studies Programs are satisfied at the reward satisfaction level, the intrinsic satisfaction level, and the concomitant satisfaction level in their positions in Black Studies. (2) In the category of educational achievement, directors of Black Studies Programs achieved 35 percent higher than their stated levels of expectations and aspirations. (3) While the directors of Black Studies Programs were basically satisfied with their positions, and while the directors' expectations and aspirations were very much related, the career orientation had no significant effect upon their job satisfaction.

161. Becknell, Charles. "Can Black Studies Survive on a Predominantly White University Campus?" Unpublished Doctoral Dissertation, University of New Mexico, 1975. 176 pp.

Dr. Becknell suggests that Black Studies Programs, in most cases, were published on the heels of Black Student activism and the demands that followed. Black Studies Programs are distinctive in several respects; the way they were organized, the special problems they had to relate to, the development of curriculum, the selection of faculty and staff and their approaches to bridging the gap between campus and community. While not all Black Studies Programs were ushered in by confrontations, the confrontation tactics influenced the development of Black Studies Programs all across the nation. As a result of the helter-skelter development of Black Studies Programs by institutions who were only trying to avoid violence, Black Studies Programs have been plagued by many problems. The major problem facing Black Studies today is the problem of how to survive on a predominantly white university campus. In today's times of budget cuts, student apathy and a re-evaluation of admission standards, survival for Black Studies becomes an extremely critical issue, argues the writer. Black Studies has been marked by a lack of cohesion and coordination in curriculum design and research. At the present time (1975) there is no national coordinating body to provide direction or technical assistance for Black Studies. As a result, there is very little consistency in the

notion as to what a Black Studies Program should do or the services
it should provide, states the author. Dr. Becknell concludes:
Black Studies Programs should operate as autonomous units, either
as departments, programs or divisions that utilize the interdisciplinary approach. These programs should be supported by "hard"
money with substantial increases each year. Black Studies Programs
also should pose a positive challenge to the traditional educational
system. The Black presence in American society can no longer be
ignored and Black Studies can assist the educational system to meet
the special needs of Black Americans.

162. Butler, Johnnella E. "Black Studies: Pedagogy and Revolution. A
     Study of Afro-American Studies and The Liberal Arts Tradition
     Through the Discipline of Afro-American Literature." Unpublished
     Doctoral Dissertation, University of Massachusetts, 1979. 182 pp.

     This dissertation offers a conceptual framework for the criticism
     and teaching of Afro-American literature, and proposes a liberating
     pedagogy developed through (1) the recognition and examination of
     the sensibility of the literature and aesthetic criticism by Afro-
     Americans which is replete with manifestations of the contradic-
     tions of the duality and of the cultural flaw, and (2) a tapping
     of student sensibility and the cultural flaw through dialogue.
     This pedagogy puts into motion a process of the raising of critica
     consciousness which affects comprehension and ultimately yields
     conscientization, states Dr. Butler.

163. Byrd, Carrie M. "Teacher Participation in the Development of an
     Elementary Black Studies Curriculum in a Suburban Setting." Un-
     published Doctoral Dissertation, Harvard University, 1976. 110 pp.

     This report is a description and analysis of a Black Studies curri-
     culum project which was coordinated by Dr. Byrd led to the comple-
     tion, field-testing and revision of an elementary Black Studies
     curriculum for the Newton Public Schools. This project centered
     on the involvement of teachers as a means of enhancing their pro-
     fessional role and on the efficacy of the use of a cognitive ap-
     proach to the teaching of Black Studies in a suburban, largely
     white, but integrating setting. A secondary concern of the project
     was the retention of system-wide administrative support for Black
     Studies curriculum development beyond the present phase until cur-
     ricula have been developed and established for all grade levels,
     K-12. Dr. Byrd suggests that a cognitive approach to Black Studies
     is more suitable than an affective approach in a largely white or
     integrating setting; that teacher participation in the process of
     curriculum development enhances the professional role of the tea-
     cher; that Action Research, with specified limitations, is useful
     technique for curriculum developers; and that the future of Black
     Studies in Newton is contingent upon the ultimate reaction of the
     top administrators to the challenge to their programmatic authority
     by the school committee, concludes the author.

164. Carey, Phillip. "The Relationship Between Black Studies, Self-Concept, and Academic Performance of Black Students on White Campuses in the Southwest." Unpublished Doctoral Dissertation, Oklahoma State University, 1975. 150 pp.

The purpose of this study was to investigate the nature of the relationship between the self-conception and academic performance of Black students on white campuses who participated in Black Studies in relation to those who did not participate. Two hundred and eighteen Black college students - undergraduates and graduates, male and female without restriction on age - were surveyed on five state university campuses in the Southwest to obtain measures of the self-concept and academic performance. Dr. Carney concludes that there was no significant difference between the level of self-concept and academic performance of Black students who participated in Black Studies and those who did not participate. The hypotheses of significant differences between participants and nonparticipants were rejected. The data indicated further that there was no correlation between measures of self-concept and of academic performance; and the hypothesis of significant difference in the self-concept and academic performance was rejected. The hypothesis that there was a significant difference in the self-concept among students attending schools with high, medium and low quality structure Black Studies Programs was rejected because of a lack of statistical evidence. Significant differences were found between three of the four measures of academic performance; therefore, the hypothesis that there was a significant difference in measures of academic performance among students at the schools with high, medium or low quality programs was supported. Further analysis indicated that the participants in Black Studies differed from the nonparticipants in that they were older single males from families of low to moderate incomes who lived in large cities, and who had serious involvement with the criminal justice system, argues the writer.

165. Carpenter, Marie Elizabeth. "The Treatment of the Negro in American History School Textbooks: A Comparison of Changing Textbook Content, 1826 to 1939, With Developing Scholarship in the History of the Negro in the United States." Unpublished Doctoral Dissertation, Columbia University, 1941. 137 pp.

The author argued more than forty-three years ago: "One of the great injustices perpetrated by public school teaching of American history has been the lack of concern or treatment of the role of the American Negro in the shaping of that history. Where he has not been ignored, the Black man has been unfortunately portrayed as a totally passive, ignorant and infantile figure who made no worthwhile contributions to America's growth and development...."

166. Chappelle, Yvonne. "Black Studies: Seeking to Renew My Connection with the University." Unpublished Doctoral Dissertation, Union Graduate School, 1974. 128 pp.

Black studies is an attempt by African-Americans to understand their African cultural heritage and value system. The goals of

Black studies are: (1) to enable a reevaluation of information from a perspective which takes into account traditional African humanistic values; (2) to encourage creativity motivated by a positive understanding of one's African-American value construction; and thereby (3) to replace the socially instilled, negative self-concept of African-Americans by a positive one, toward more effective social functioning. A sound Black studies program must take fully into account this premise and its logical corollaries, argues the author. Dr. Chappelle concludes: "Black studies must help us understand the implications of these differences for our pedagogy. We may one day discover that much of the poor performance on the part of Black children in school has to do with cultural conflict - a basic difference between values learned at home and those required at school."

167. Colon, Alan K. "A Critical Review of Black Studies Programs." Unpublished Doctoral Dissertation, Stanford University, 1980. 206 pp.

According to Dr. Colon the modern Afro-American liberation has been accompanied by the search for and realization of educational alternatives for Black people. This movement has been punctuated by a pivotal problem: How can an oppressed group create and sustain a form of education that will be liberating for the group in a social-political-economic order that emphasizes individual success as a prime value and is, therefore, antagonistic to a group liberation ethnic value system? Black Studies was proposed as a theoretical critique and practical departure from the racist-elitist aspects of Euro-American scholarship and schooling, declares the author. As a specific liberation-oriented outgrowth of a general tradition of Afro-centric scholarship among Black Americans, Black Studies emerged as an attempt at favorably impacting on the fundamental dilemma posed by the question above. Dr. Colon suggests that toward addressing that problem, a number of related sub-questions can be raised which have been neglected or insufficiently treated in the existing Black Studies literature: (1) What are its prevailing developmental issues and evaluative concerns? (2) What paradigms for successful organization and operation can be identified? (3) What projections, in light of Black liberation goals, can be made for the future of Black Studies? The writer argues that while the effort at course standardization, especially at the introductory level, is underway, a concomitant need exists to establish a coherent philosophy of Afro-American education which Black Studies could serve. Individual programs must crystallize their mission and specialize more around their strengths. Programs of doctoral study are urgently needed to supply the field with scholars who will advance it. A Black Studies research agenda is needed as is a broadly-supported single publication for the field. A viable national organization is also a priority. Stronger linkages must be created among programs on Black and white campuses with community-based Black enterprises. Finally, the survival and growth of Black Studies is related to and dependent upon the extent to which the larger liberation aspirations of Black people are fulfilled, concludes the author.

168. Connolly, Michael N. "Students' and Teachers' Opinions of the Existing Programs for the Study of Black Americans in Michigan High School Social Studies Curriculums." Unpublished Doctoral Dissertation, Michigan State University, 1972. 201 pp.

The purpose of this study was to locate existing programs in Michigan high school social studies curriculums that specifically dealt with the study of Black Americans, and to survey students' and teachers' opinions concerning these programs. Dr. Connolly argues: (1) A majority (63.6%) of the high school social studies programs in counties in southern and central Michigan specifically included the study of Black Americans. (2) Schools with larger percentages of Black students were more likely to specifically include the study of Black Americans. (3) Schools with larger percentages of Black students were more likely to offer a separate course primarily concerned with the study of Black Americans. (4) Students as a group were negative when responding to statements concerning their school's social studies program for the study of Black Americans. (5) There was no significant difference between students' responses in schools that offered a separate course and students' responses in schools that specifically included the study of Black Americans, but did not offer a separate course. (6) Students were most positive towards statements which dealt with: expression of opinions in class; the adequacy of the library; analyzing racial issues important to them; the general treatment of the study of Black Americans in social studies; and the adequacy of audio-visual aids.

169. Crawford, Zelte. "The Effects of Black Studies Exposure on Racial Consciousness and Black Self-Concept." Unpublished Doctoral Dissertation, Stanford University, 1979. 170 pp.

This study is an attempt to test whether Black self-concept can be positively affected by re-education. By adapting a Marxism model of consciousness, Black Studies is treated for its effects on self-concept. Dr. Crawford concludes: "Consciousness and self-concept are affected by a number of factors but Black Studies is positively related to racial consciousness and self-concept mainly by increasing awareness of Black History and culture and promoting positive racial identity and community efficacy."

170. Curtis, Willie M. "Enhancing Black Self-Concept Through Black Studies." Unpublished Doctoral Dissertation, University of Arizona, 1975. 127 pp.

The purpose of this study was to assess the effectiveness of a structured Black Studies program on the self-concepts of Black youth. The focus of the program was to increase cultural awareness through the use of historical and literary material, and through exposure to achievement models. Black history and literature were chosen as they provide models for identification, new positive role perceptions for highlighting Black contributions and vehicles for understanding and articulating the Black experience. Subjects were 50 low SES adolescents from Tucson, Arizona, and East Palo Alto, California, who were assigned to either Black Studies, Consultation

Rapping Control, or No-Treatment Control conditions. Dr. Curtis
suggests that Black Studies subjects manifested significant increase from pretest to post-test on the Total Positive (an index of
the general level of self-esteem) and identification scores. Con-
sultation/Rapping Control subjects manifested a significant increase
from pretest to post-test on the Total Positive score. There were
no other significant within-or between-group differences. Black
self-concept is a multi-dimensional entity. Cultural and ethnic
identity are two very important constituents of self-esteem.
There are numerous others, e.g., personal identity, interpersonal
interaction, etc. Consideration of these will facilitate self-
concept enhancement. Black Studies is seen as a viable method of
enhancing Black self-concept, concludes the author.

171. Daniel, Phillip T. "The Relationships Between Black Studies Cour-
     ses and the Attitudinal Change in Black and White University
     Student." Unpublished Doctoral Dissertation, University of Illinois
     at Urbana-Champaign, 1973. 106 pp.

The purpose of this study was to examine the attitudinal affects
of Black Studies on Black and White university students. Attitudinal effects referred to changes in Black students' self-concepts
and changes in white students' attitudes towards Blacks. Theories
of relevance, evaluations of instructors and grades on content
exams were also examined. The results tended to support the hypothesis that Black students who did better on the content exams improved their self-concept moreso than Black students who did not
do so well on the content exams. The hypothesis that Black students who saw the Black Studies courses as relevant would have a
better self-concept than those who saw the course as less relevant
was not supported. It was found that Black students' attitudes
towards themselves, their race and white people changed considerab-
ly as a result of the Black Studies courses. Data from the white
students showed similar findings. It was determined that there
was a definite improvement in what whites thought of Black people
after taking the course. Further analysis showed that there was
no significant difference between the self-concepts of Blacks and
whites. At the same time, there were no significant differences
in how they rated Black people. However, there was a great difference in how they rated White people. The evaluation whites
gave was good; the one Blacks gave was poor. Dr. Daniel concludes
from this data that Black Studies courses can be a determining
agent in the attitudes of both Black and white students in an
educational setting.

172. Darmstadt, Margaret A. "The Effects of a Verbal Intervention in
     Black and Social Studies Courses on Locus of Control Ideology,
     Cognitive Dissonance and Militant Attitudes." Unpublished Doctoral
     Dissertation, Rutgers University, 1972. 106 pp.

This study investigated the effects of verbal intervention on cognitive dissonance, locus of control and militant attitudes on four
groups of high school students. This study used field conditions
and attempted to avoid experimental manipulation of the subjects

as much as possible. The subjects, all juniors or seniors in high
school, were chosen from two Black Studies classes taught by one
teacher and two Social Studies classes taught by another. The test
was administered by the respective teachers within the context of
the class period. It was found that for the dissonance variable a
significant interaction occurred between curriculum and treatment
effects alone accounted for a significant amount of the change.
Intervention reduced dissonance in the Black Studies group whereas
it increased it in the Social Studies group. The combination of
the Black Studies and treatment was the most effective in reducing
dissonance. The main effect in the militancy variable was also the
unique combination of Black Studies and intervention. Only this
condition showed a significant reduction of military scores. No
significant change was shown in any of the four conditions for the
internal control variable by either analysis of variance or tests,
observed Dr. Darmstadt. A possible explanation offered for the
findings was that intervention and Black Studies decreased the students' sense of powerlessness, thereby decreasing dissonance and
militancy. Internal control, on the other hand, was viewed as a
core personality construct and as such, it was not subject to mea-
surable modifiability through limited intervention, concludes Dr.
Darmstadt.

173. Davis, Clifford L. "Black Student Movements and Their Influence
in Ten High Schools in the Los Angeles City Unified School District." Unpublished Doctoral Dissertation, University of California at Los Angeles, 1971. 171 pp.

This study determined the influence of Black student movements in
curricula, programs, activities, and administrative policies and
practices in ten selected high schools in the Los Angeles City
unified School District and to determine the extent of degree of
their influence. The conclusions, based on the data from the
study, were: (1) Black courses, once added, were seldom dropped
from curricula. (2) Black students and their parents participated
more actively in curriculum decision making between 1960 and 1970.
(3) There is a trend toward fewer ethnic courses with integration
of units on Blacks, and other ethnic minorities, into regular courses. (4) The functioning of non-school Black organizations directly affected Black student movements leading to the formation of
Black Student Unions in all ten schools. (5) Black student groups
influenced the development of new programs in all ten schools and
will continue to be a factor. (6) Non-school Black organizations
influenced Black student groups to engage in unauthorized activities in all ten schools. (7) Actual membership in Black Student
Unions was less than 5 percent of the student body in each of the
ten schools. (8) The Black Students Alliance was the most influen-
tial non-school group in the selected schools. (9) Demands for
changes in certain rules and policies were presented to administrators in all of the selected schools. (10) The number of Black teachers and administrators in the selected schools increased as the
number of Black students increased.

174. Dorsey, Carolyn A. "Role Expectations For the Black Studies Program Director." Unpublished Doctoral Dissertation, New York University, 1976. 200 pp.

The purpose of the study was to compare expectations for the role
of Black Studies Program Director (BSPD) held by the BSPD with
those held by selected role-set groups, i.e., the administrator
under whom the BSPD worked directly, faculty of the program, student majors, "other students" defined as non majors taking Black
Studies courses and members of Black student campus groups, and
community people who related to the BSPD or Black Studies program.
The mechanisms that the BSPD used to accommodate to differences
were also explored, as were other expectations held for the BSPD
by the respondents. The sample was a stratified random sample of
ten BSPD's and their role-set members from predominantly white
institutions in New York, New Jersey and Pennsylvania. Three instruments were constructed to collect data: the "Black Studies
Program Director's Interview Schedule," "Black Studies Program
Director's Role Description Questionnaire". Significant differences were found between the BSPD and the administrator, but not between the BSPD and the "other students", the BSPD and the faculty,
and the BSPD and the majors on the Admin Scale: between the BSPD
BSPD and the "other students", and between the BSPD and majors but
not between the BSPD and the administrator and the BSPD and the
faculty on the Faculty Scale; and between the BSPD and the administrator but not between the BSPD and the other role-set members on
the StuCom Scale. It was found that friction resulting from differences was most often held at a minimum by the groups meeting
and "ironing out" differences. Dr. Dorsey concludes that BSPD
should establish an accountability system to insure that students
are receiving effective instruction, raise funds for scholarships,
identify sources of funds for students, counsel students, have ties
with other Third World Programs, be primarily an administrator, and
investigate charges of racism.

175. Duke, William D. "The Conceptual Problems Involved in Developing
a Structural and Academically Approved Study of Black People in
Relation to the Establishment of a Curriculum in Black Studies."
Unpublished Doctoral Dissertation, Northwestern University, 1973.
147 pp.

Dr. Duke studied the backgrounds of a certain number of upward mo-
bile Blacks (Group A) and an equal number of underachieving Blacks
(Group B) and compared and assessed experience factors in their
backgrounds on an individual basis. The purpose was to determine
whether collective experiences in either group contained a certain
pattern which differed from the experiences of the White society.
The results of the study were analyzed and used as part of the
discussion of conceptual problems involved in developing a structural and academically approved study of Black people for consideration for use in a Black curriculum. The author concludes that a
properly constructed curriculum of Black studies, within the most
effective context, is a necessity. The place to begin is in the
established centers of education with teachers who have accountability and dedication to give students the assistance they need to

use studies such as these to promulgate solutions to the Black
"problem". And with such an approach, hopefully, the students'
environment will be more meaningful to them, and, as adults, they
will be better prepared to help ameliorate racial problems and racial polarization, asserts the author.

176. Filter, Paul A. "Blacks Studies in the Secondary Social Studies
Curriculum Position and Opinions". Unpublished Doctoral Dissertation, University of Nebraska-Lincoln, 1970. 180 pp.

The purpose of this study was to determine the position of, and influences, concerning Black Studies in the social studies curriculum of secondary schools in the North Central Association. The
study specifically attempted to discover how many schools had a
Black Studies program, when it had been adopted, why it had, or had
not been adopted, the criteria for selecting Black Studies instructors, and whether student interests in Black Studies had increased
or decreased. The study also attempted to determine the opinions
of social studies department chairmen concerning Black Studies.
Dr. Filter arrived at eight conclusions: (1) Most Black students
in the North Central Association were concentrated in metropolitan
schools that had Black Studies programs, and those schools spent
longer periods of time on Black Studies than non-metropolitan
schools. (2) Approximately one-half of the secondary schools with
an enrollment of over 1,000 students in the North Central Association had a Black Studies program. (3) Respondents overwhelmingly
agreed it was a legitimate part of social studies to place special
emphasis on the contributions of Blacks. (4) Nine-tenths of the
Blacks Studies programs in the North Central Association were started in the period from 1967-1969. The study also indicated there
may be a leveling off of the growth of Black Studies. (5) Social
Studies teachers have not been well prepared to teach Black Studies,
and textbooks are of limited use. However, supplementary materials
were considered adequate by respondents. (6) There was a complete
rejection by respondents of demands by militants in the teaching
of Black Studies. (7) There was agreement that the most important
objective in teaching Black Studies was to accurately portray the
history of Black Americans. (8) Most social studies department
chairmen were sympathetic to Black Studies.

177. Fisher, David L. "Black Studies and the Enhancement of Self-
Concept as it Relates to Achievement Level in Negro High School
Students." Unpublished Doctoral Dissertation, Western Michigan
University, 1972. 85 pp.

This study had as its primary purpose the investigation of the
effect of Black Studies courses upon the self-concept of Negro
high school students. Specifically, it was intended to determine
if self-concept enhancement followed completion of Black Studies
courses and if this enhancement effect was further related to
prior academic achievement. A secondary purpose was to determine
if self-concept enhancement was related to the sex of the student.
There were two subsidiary purposes. One was to see if different
Black Studies courses had different effects upon the self-concept

of the students and the other was to determine if the four instruments were used independent measurements of differing aspects of
the self-concept, stated Dr. Fisher. He concludes that while Black
Studies might have self-concept enhancement effects that they did
not affect all the measured aspects of self-concept and that the
effects were not always in the desired direction. Black Studies,
as a curriculum tool for self-concept enhancement, should be ap-
proached with caution. The instruments used did measure different
aspects of self-concept and that one course, Afro-American History,
had a greater effect upon self-concept than did Black Literature,
the other Black Studies course, observed the author.

178. Flamer, Richard E. "A Study of Selected Factors Relevant to the
     Continuation of Black Studies Programs in Four-Year Colleges and
     Universities in the United States." Unpublished Doctoral Disser-
     tation, Gonzaga University, 1983. 138 pp.

     This work identified, described and compared some of the factors
     existing in Black Studies programs in the United States. The au-
     thor states that the major findings of the study indicated that
     the majority of program directors had control over individual bud-
     gets and had sufficient funds to order new research materials; the
     majority of programs were no longer experiencing difficulty in lo-
     cating and hiring academically qualified faculty; a majority
     of units did not have a structural tutorial program to assist
     Black Students; and all institutions had a counseling center with a
     majority reporting a Black counselor on their staffs. A majority
     of programs did not sponsor a separate orientation program for in-
     coming new Black students; a majority of units were funded by in-
     stitutional funds and considered their funding level to be compara-
     ble with other academic departments. Dr. Flamer concludes that
     this study appears to indicate that Black Studies are firmly en-
     trenched as a part of the academic community; that Black Studies
     faculty are as well qualified academically as their counterparts in
     traditional departments; that library resources are of sufficient
     depth to support adequately the academic preparation required for
     Black studies course work. Separate orientation for incoming Black
     Studies supported tutorial programs did not appear to be signifi-
     cant factors in the continuation of Black Studies programs.

179. Fleet, Clara M. "Attitudes of Black Undergraduate Students Toward
     Black Studies." Unpublished Doctoral Dissertation, Catholic Uni-
     versity of America, 1974. 193 pp.

     The purpose of this study was to determine the attitudes of selec-
     ted Black undergraduate students toward Black Studies. In an ana-
     lysis of the problem, specific subproblems were isolated and became
     the basis for the investigation. Dr. Fleet argues that there was
     no significant difference in the attitudes of students registered
     in Black Studies and students not registered in Black Studies. Nor
     was there a significant difference in attitudes between the sexes
     or in students majoring in Black Studies. Based on minor grada-
     tions in average weights, it was noted that the more positive atti-
     tudes were held by the 24 to 26 year age group, the seniors and

juniors, those exposed to Black Studies in high school and those whose parental income was between $4,000 to $6,000 per annum, concludes the author.

180. Ford, Luther Lee. "A National Survey of Degree-Granting Black Studies Programs." Unpublished Doctoral Dissertation, University of Nebraska-Lincoln, 1974. 140 pp.

This work assessed the functions and the effectiveness of Afro-American and Black Studies degree-granting programs in American colleges and universities. Specifically, this survey focused on examining some of the problems of Afro-American and Black Studies degree-granting programs. The author concludes that psychologically, Black Studies have helped Black students to become more aware of Black identity, history and culture. Sociologically, Black students have become more involved in campus affairs. Ideologically, Black students have become more concerned about other Black people in other parts of the world. The majority of Black Studies faculty members have master's degrees but less than seven years of teaching experience. Administrators and faculty members generally cooperate to improve Black Studies degree-granting institutions, observed Dr. Ford.

181. Frye, Charles A. "The Impact of Black Studies on the Undergraduate Curricula of English and Selected Social Sciences at Three Universities". Unpublished Doctoral Dissertation, University of Pittsburgh, 1976. 117 pp.

The question investigated was whether Black Studies had had substantial impact on traditional social science disciplines and English as perceived by chairpersons or departments in those disciplines. The findings indicated that the major impact of the Black Studies movement and the wider activism of which it was a part has apparently not been greatly manifested in formal undergraduate curricula changes. The impact of the Black Studies movement seems to have been more informal, more subtle in nature, concludes Dr. Frye.

182. Fullwood, Nathaniel N. "An Analysis of Perceived and Stated Objectives of the Black Studies Department of the Ohio State University." Unpublished Doctoral Dissertation, Ohio State University, 1973. 333 pp.

The study identifies the perceived and stated objectives of the Black Studies Department of The Ohio State University and the relationships between the two categories of objectives as they relate to the performance measures of the department. The identification of the objectives resulted with four primary classifications of performance objectives: ideological, administrative policy, curriculum, and service objectives. The significance of the study is that it describes the role and importance of defining and setting objectives as the basis for program development, budget planning, and personnel growth and development. Further, it is essential that the organization provide for an on-going means of determining what its clientele perceives as goals and objectives, declares Dr. Fullwood. The basic assumptions and conclusions to be drawn from this dissertation are: (1) Black Studies is a field still being born; (2) establishing and defining the field of Black Studies is a task logically for Black people in America and elsewhere to undertake; (3) the Black Studies programs and departments themselves can perform an important function of defining and developing models so urgently required; (4) a unified rather than a conventional discipline around the approach to the development of Black Studies is absolutely necessary, and finally, utilizing the perceptiveness of The Institute of Black World; (5) a serious building of this field is the task of years and not a makeshift program for a few persons to do in several weeks or months.

183. Giles, Raymond H., Jr. "Black and Ethnic Studies Programs at Public Schools: Elementary and Secondary." Unpublished Doctoral Dissertation, University of Massachusetts, 1972. 379 pp.

Operating on the premise that the public schools are the major purveyors of American traditions and cultures and therefore that racial prejudice and discrimination should be addressed through the educational system this study examined the operations of various ethnic and Black Studies programs and their impact on racial attitudes. The major purpose of the study was to collect data and information related to the assessment and improvement of these programs in order to propose new strategies and more relevant content and approaches for in-service teacher education programs, establish new projects in the public schools, and evaluate the impact and effectiveness of such programs. Contributionism, Black identity, and a thematic approach emerged as three distinct approaches to the teaching of Black studies. The study raises a number of questions calling for varied interpretations and definitions of a Black Studies, a look at the origin and sponsorship of Black Studies as well as the need for clarifying their purposes within diverse settings, and who should teach and who should take Black Studies as well as the need for broader representation of interests and student needs in the development of each program. Much of the solution seems to be in teacher preparation. Curriculum reform and adequate evaluation techniques for measuring the impact and effectiveness of Black Studies programs are also discussed as well as alternatives to the educational problems to which Black Studies are considered panaceas, concludes Dr. Giles.

184. Goggin, Jacqueline Ann. "Carter G. Woodson and The Movement To Promote Black History." Unpublished Doctoral Dissertation, University of Rochester, 1984. 416 pp.

According to Dr. Goggin, Carter G. Woodson pioneered in the study of Black history in numerous ways. He held annual meetings of the Association for the Study of Negro Life and History, collected source materials, edited and published the Journal of Negro History and The Negro History Bulletin, established the Associated Publishers, and wrote and edited dozens of books, articles, and reviews. Because of his lifetime commitment to Black History and the high

scholarly standards he formulated, Woodson was able to attract financial support for Association activities. Thus, the formation
of the Association was the first step towards institutionalized inquiry in Black History, states the author. Woodson championed
more than the writing of history that accurately reflected the
Black past. He maintained that Blacks were miseducated because
Black educational systems promoted white middle class culture.
Woodson reached a large audience of Afro-Americans through the establishment of a systematic program of organized research, publications, and celebrations that involved both scholarly and popular
audiences, concludes Dr. Goggin.

185. Hagan, Lee F. "Black Studies Programs: An Analysis of Curricula."
Unpublished Doctoral Dissertation, Rutgers University, The State
University of New Jersey, 1983. 101 pp.

The purpose of this study was to examine the development and changes that took place in Black Studies curricula at four year col-
legiate institutions in New Jersey from their inception to 1982.
The study began with an historical analysis of the status of Black
Studies from the Colonial period to contemporary times and the institutionalization of the Black Experience in higher education.
Five institutions, based upon criteria established by the researcher, were selected for the study: Princeton University, Seton Hall
University, Trenton State College, Upsala College, and William
Paterson College. All five programs in this study reflect their
own evolutionary process, which was influenced by the setting,
political climate, and resources available for implementation and
development. Retrenchment in legislative appropriations for higher education and declining enrollments have retarded the growth of
the Black Studies curriculum. Other salient factors which emerged
from this study included: the transition from loosely coordinated
programs to autonomous or quasi-departmental entities; the dramatic increase in the number and diversity of courses; the influence
of socio-political events upon the curriculum; greater attention
to research methodology; more coverage of Africa and the Caribbean;
and the lack of viable community-based curriculum. Within the li-
mitations of this study, the researcher provided information and
models which could be useful for developing curricular programs in
Black Studies and other ethnic studies programs.

186. Harris, Ann B. "A Descriptive Study of the Supportive Instruction
Program of The Black Studies Institute at Ohio University." Unpublished Doctoral Dissertation, Ohio University, 1970. 135 pp.

The Black Studies Institute's Supportive Instruction Program at
Ohio University, Athens, Ohio, provided supplemental instruction
to poorly academically-prepared Black students in the Freshman
class of 1969. The purpose of this study was to evaluate the Supportive Instruction Program. Dr. Harris arrived at the following
conclusions: (1) Apparently Supportive Instruction makes it possible for the tutored-Black freshman to make better grades than
the non-tutored-Black freshmen. (2) Grades the tutored-Black
students make are not dependent upon the amount of time these students spend with a Supportive Instructor. (4) Almost all of the

tutored-Black freshmen feel that their Supportive Instructors have good or excellent knowledge of the subject matter. (5) A majority of the tutored-Black freshmen feel that they are making passing grades based on their receiving a sufficient amount of help. (6) The sample of non-tutored-Black freshmen do not appear as definite about seeking help through Supportive Instruction the next quarter as do the students who are receiving the help through the Program. (7) All of the tutored and non-tutored-Black freshmen express positive feelings about having such a program, and feel that it should be continued and expanded. The Supportive Instructors indicate this by the large number of students they say they are advising to continue to seek help through Supportive Instruction the following quarter.

187. Harris, Jeanette H. "Black Studies: A Challenge to the American Education System." Unpublished Doctoral Dissertation, University of Massachusetts, 1974. 205 pp.

The aim of this study was to examine and to evaluate the effectiveness of the Black Studies program at Classical High School in Springfield, Massachusetts, as it evolved and developed from September 1969 through June 1973. The study, primarily based within a classroom setting, proposed a strategy which would describe and compare factors involved in the development of the program. The factors - goals, students, curricular design, social climate, and, to an extent, school personnel - had varying influences on the evolving program. The Black Studies program moved through four phases. The study concluded with an evaluation of Classical's Black Studies program. Major issues dealt with concern, Black and White student disinterest and other teacher disinterest. Attempts were made not only to understand the basis of each program encountered, but also to suggest a possible solution to the particular situation. Furthermore, conclusions were made with regard to the value and the direction of Black Studies at Classical. The program seemed to be of nominal effectiveness in the Springfield setting. The extent to which Black Studies - applied as a change agent to help eradicate racism - could penetrate the educating process would be limited until more classroom educators were better prepared to deal with the Black experience, asserts Dr. Harris.

188. Harrison, Daphne M. "An Exploitation Study of Three Curricular Approaches to Black Studies and Their Effect on the Acceptance of Blackness by Middle-Grades Pupils." Unpublished Doctoral Dissertation, University of Miami, 1971. 221 pp.

This was an exploratory investigation of the effects of three curricular approaches to Black Studies on the dimension of Black acceptance. Black acceptance is viewed here as a dynamic component of the self-concept. Three types of curricula were designed and administered which centered on protest movements in America. One was an integrated social studies course which mentioned Blacks only where they appeared in historical chronology. The second treatment was a history course on Black protest in America. The third treatment was a contemporary view of protest as it exists in

the Black community. Treatments one and two were taught by one
classroom teacher. Treatment three was taught by a variety of
Blacks who were or had been involved in social protest recently,
states Mrs. Harrison. According to Dr. Harrison, the reader is
cautioned not to make judgment for or against Black Studies in curriculum and the objectives sought should be understood in relation
to the type of student body and staff which would be involved.

189. Hayden, Barbara L. "Purpose of Black Higher Education As Viewed
by Black College Faculty and Black Studies Faculty." Unpublished
Doctoral Dissertation, University of Pittsburgh, 1978.   155 pp.

The purpose of this study was to assess the views of Black college
faculty and Black Studies faculty about eight potential purposes
of Black higher education, each related to change in the individual and/or in society. The study was based on the assumption
that both Black colleges and Black Studies can be perceived as components of one entity, Black higher education. A second assumption
of the study was that the quest for change in the individual and/
or in society is a strong enough theme in the literature in Black
higher education to warrant its investigation. Dr. Hayden observes that a review of some of the 1969-1977 literature in Black
higher education produced eight recurrent themes relating to change
in the individual and/or in society: (1) To prepare the student
to compete effectively in a competitive heirarchical economic system. (2) To prepare the student to help promote an economic system that is cooperative rather than competitive. (3) To assimilate
the student into the dominant culture. (4) To foster racial soli-
darity. (5) To prepare the student to live in a pluralistic society. (6) To develop a commitment to serve the Black community.
(7) To enhance the self-concept of the student. (8) To help bring
about self-determination. The writer believes that the Black Studies faculty tended to give substantially lower ratings to Purpose 3 (to assimilate the student into the dominant culture) than
to the other seven. Dr. Hayden concludes that the data also are
interpreted to mean that there is general agreement between Black
college faculty and Black Studies faculty that the other seven
purposes are important goals of Black higher education, although
the exact order of importance may be viewed differently by the
two faculty groups.

190. Henderson, Dale E. "A Story of Opinions Concerning the Integration of Black History Into the History or Social Science Curricula
in The University of North Carolina." Unpublished Doctoral Dissertation, George Washington University, 1983.   165 pp.

The purpose of this study was to survey the opinions of selected
administrators and American and Black history teachers in the fif-
teen constituent institutions of the University of North Carolina
regarding the integration of Black history into the history or social science curriculum of their institutions. The study revealed that there was no significant difference between the opinions
of the respondents. They overwhelmingly concurred that Black history should be integrated into American history, and approximately

two-thirds also felt the need for separate Black history courses,
stated the writer. Among the eleven recommendations made, the
following are major ones according to Dr. Henderson: (1) Black
history should be fully integrated into American history courses;
(2) separate Black history courses should be made available to interested students; (3) special effort should be made through committee action to identify, review, and select Black history materials to supplement American history courses, as well as separate
Black history courses; (4) the University System should bring
pressure to bear on publishers of textbooks and materials on American history to publish works that truly represent America and all
its people on an equitable basis; and (5) further research should
be conducted in other universities and in school systems in order
to provide a broad perspective on the subject of Black history.

191. Horton, Harold. "A Study of the Status of Black Studies in Uni-
     versities and Colleges in the United States." Unpublished Docto-
     ral Dissertation, Ohio State University, 1974. 193 pp.

     The purpose of the study was to determine the current status of
     Black Studies programs at accredited universities and colleges in
     the United States. More specifically, the author attempted to an-
     swer questions relative to the origin, educational objectives, or-
     ganizational structure, personnel, course offerings, crucial prob-
     lems, and trends of Black Studies programs at institutions of high-
     er education. Dr. Horton made the following conclusions: that
     the meaningful involvement of students and community members in
     Black Studies programs has set a precedent by which other areas
     can benefit; that such programs are, for the most part, academical-
     ly sound in their cognitive orientation; that more financial sup-
     port must be forthcoming if the programs are to thrive; and that
     those seeking positions in Black Studies must have graduate equi-
     valent to those of faculty members at large. It was evident from
     the study that administrators for academic affairs must assume a
     more overt leadership role in assessing and refining Afro-American
     Studies programs in order that the vitality and academic legiti-
     macy of such programs be ensured, declares the author.

192. Hulbary, William E. "Adolescent Political Self-Images and Politi-
     cal Involvement: The Relative Effects of High School Black Studies
     Courses and Prior Socialization." Unpublished Doctoral Disserta-
     tion, University of Iowa, 1972. 233 pp.

     This study examined the influence of Black Studies courses and
     some indicators of prior socialization on adolescent political
     self-images and predispositions to engage in two different kinds
     of political activity - partisan activism and political dissent.
     According to Dr. Hulbary the findings do not suggest that new and
     unfamiliar political information provided by Black Studies courses
     was an important determinant of political self-images and politi-
     cal activism. The influence of other social studies courses,
     though also modest, was as great as or greater than that of Black
     Studies courses and extended to a wider range of variables. Nor
     do the findings indicate that other social studies courses had

equally strong effects on political self-images and orientations
toward activism, concludes Dr. Hulbary.

193. Irvine, Freeman R., Jr.   "An Analysis of Black Studies Programs
     in Black Colleges Within the Southeastern United States with Re-
     commendations for a Masters Degree Program." Unpublished Doctoral
     Dissertation, University of Tennessee, 1972.   149 pp.

     The purpose of this study was to analyze selected Black Studies
     programs at six Black colleges and/or universities in the south-
     eastern United States, and to make recommendations regarding the
     design of a graduate program of studies dealing with the Black
     American for Florida A & M University. The findings of this study
     showed that there are only five Black colleges and universities in
     the southeastern United States offering a degree of any kind in
     Black studies. Further, the findings showed that the majority of
     Black Studies programs on Black campuses in the southeastern United
     States are interdisciplinary in nature, and that these programs
     are open to both Black and white students. Another of the major
     findings of this study showed that a majority of the administrators
     of these Black Studies programs believe that the staff for Black
     Studies should be selected on the basis of what they have to offer
     the school, the program, and the student, without regard to race,
     color or academic credentials, and that any masters degree program
     in Black Studies should include community experiences in the Black
     community and some form of research dealing with the Black Ameri-
     cans as well as many and varied classroom experiences, concludes
     Dr. Irvine.

194. Issac, Amos.   "The Development and Status of Black and Brown Stu-
     dies at the Claremont Colleges: The University of California at
     Riverside, California State College at San Bernardino and San
     Bernardino Valley Community College, and University College/John-
     ston College in Redlands, 1967-1972, A Cross Comparison." Un-
     published Doctoral Dissertations, Claremont Graduate School, 1972.
     384 pp.

     According to Dr. Issac any college that responds to the demands
     for the institution of Black and Brown Studies becomes embroiled
     in the issue of organizational change. This study was equally
     concerned with the nature of organizations and of various models
     for implementing change in organizations. Related to this is the
     central issue of the cultural role of colleges, states the author.
     Dr. Issac concludes: (1) that any attempt to categorize any eth-
     nic group as all of one mind or that there cannot be legitimate
     differences of opinions by members of a given ethnic group, is a
     fallacy; (2) that an attempt to evaluate the adequacy of a res-
     ponse to organizational change by a single model has inherent
     weaknesses; (3) that a knowledge of the historical and social ways
     that a given group had dealt with organizations is essential to
     any viable evaluation of the effectiveness of their encounter with
     organizational change; (4) any attempt to relieve any group of the
     responsibility of aiding to achieve effective organizational change
     will be counterproductive; (5) adequate developmental monies and

due consideration to lead time is essential. One of the greatest
tendencies is to overwork ethnic studies personnel whereas what is
actually needed is more released time for developing and reasses-
sing the programs; (6) that educational institutions ought to se-
riously ask themselves the question of what it is that they need
to do that they have neglected....

195. Jackson, Florence A. "Effects of American History Including
     Black Studies on Self-Concept, Attitude, and Attendance of Lower
     Income Black Children." Unpublished Doctoral Dissertation.
     Fordham University, 1979. 113 pp.

     This study sought to determine whether or not the use of an Ameri-
     can history curriculum including Black history and culture had an
     effect on the self-concept, attitude toward social studies and at-
     tendance of fourth-grade, low-income Black children of both Ameri-
     can and Caribbean-born parents. Dr. Jackson concludes: (1) The
     results of this study supported the assumption that the use of an
     American history curriculum which includes information on Black
     history and culture improves the self-concepts of low-income
     fourth-grade Black children of American-born parents. (2) Both
     the children of American-born parents and children of Caribbean-
     born parents had a better attitude toward social studies and a
     better attendance record as a result of having Black history and
     culture included in the American history curriculum. (3) An Amer-
     ican history curriculum including Black history and culture does
     not bring about significant change in how children of Caribbean-
     born parents view themselves. Therefore, the self-concept mean
     scores of the pre-test and post-test did not show a significant
     difference at p.05. (4) The children of American-born parents and
     those of Caribbean-born parents appeared to have improved their
     attendance as a result of having Black history and culture inclu-
     ded in the American history curriculum.

196. Johnson, Jeffalyn H. "Experience and Attitudes of Black and White
     Community College Students Toward Selected Public Institutions."
     Unpublished Doctoral Dissertation, University of Southern Cali-
     fornia, 1972. 168 pp.

     The major purpose of this study was to determine the similarities
     and differences between Black and white community college students
     in their personal characteristics and in their experiences with
     and attitudes toward selected public institutions. The institu-
     tions of the armed services, law enforcement, the political pro-
     cess and education were selected for study because they are fre-
     quently the targets of student protests. According to Dr. Johnson
     these findings suggest that racism could be reduced through an
     educational process designed to dispel the myths, misconceptions,
     and distortions that serve as the foundation of racism. The find-
     ings indicate that Black Studies programs could provide information
     about, and experiences with, Black people that would foster the de-
     velopment of a more culturally pluralistic orientation in our so-
     ciety, suggests the author.

197. Kelly, Samuel E. "A Model for Emerging Black Studies Programs:
An Analysis of Selected Black Studies Programs Viewed in Historical Perspective." Unpublished Doctoral Dissertation, University
of Washington, 1971. 271 pp.

Since the death of Dr. Martin Luther King, there was a prolifera-
tion of programs seeking to address themselves to Black Studies as
a viable academic endeavor. These programs grew out of an extremely urgent and confrontive set of circumstances. As a result, mul-
titudes of Black students across the country entered programs which
were hastily assembled by faculty and administrators who were not
necessarily committed to Black morally, academically and economi-
cally. Hence, many of these programs were designed for failure,
while others limped along, states Dr. Kelly. This thesis nationally
used six universities as examples of differing programs. Primary
and secondary source materials provide empirical data which speak
in an historiographical sense to the backgrounds of these emerging
programs with a view toward program design of some depth, flexibility and durability. This study is germane to the survival of the
educational process which affects growing numbers of Black students.
The six selected universities were examined on the basis of origin,
type of academic program offered, requirements for entry to the
Black Studies program, special admission policies and supportive
services. Common difficulties encountered by the Black Studies
program included limited financial resources, problems in achieving faculty and administrative support, and ambivalence on the
part of the academic community toward moving to meet the needs of
minority peoples. Analysis revealed that some program elements at
all the universities were lacking in comprehensiveness, direction
and sequence. A model for an Ethnic Studies College and Black
Studies component of that college was developed which would address
itself to the needs of minority groups as well as non-minority students. In addition, the formation of an Office of Minority Affairs
is discussed, which would coordinate the areas of non-academic support, concludes Dr. Kelly.

198. Kent, George R. "A Survey of Integrated and Separate Black Studies in Maryland Secondary Schools, Grades 10-12." Unpublished
Doctoral Dissertation, University of Maryland, 1971. 230 pp.

Dr. Kent points out that during the decade of the 1960's, Black
Americans insisted that the curriculum of the schools failed to
reflect conditions unique to Blacks. They demanded Black Studies,
and educators responded with a variety of programs. Generally,
these programs were of two types. They provided curricular offerings in Black Studies through typical courses in the curriculum
or through separate courses designed to treat the Black experience.
This study examined integrated and separate Black Studies offerings in Maryland secondary schools, grades 10-12. The author
concludes: (1) There is a difference in curricular emphasis on
topics relevant to Black Studies between offerings integrated into
regular or typical social studies courses and those taught as separate Black Studies courses. (2) There is a difference in curricular emphases on topics related to Black Studies between schools
of varying-white racial compositions.

199. Kiah, Donald A. "An Identification of Black Studies Programs In
the State of Maryland With Emphasis On The Black Studies Program
in the Public High Schools of Prince Georges County, Maryland, As
Perceived By Principals, Teachers and Students in the Spring Semes-
ter of 1970-71." Unpublished Doctoral Dissertation, George Washington University, 1972. 271 pp.

1. The purpose of this study was to identify the current status
of Black Studies programs in the State of Maryland and more specifically to examine how the program was perceived by principals,
teachers and students in Prince Georges County. The study focused
attention on the following areas: (1) curriculum, (2) personnel,
(3) organization, and (4) evaluation. Dr. Kiah came to these conclusions: 1. The state, by means of policy and legislation, was
found to have provided for programs dealing with the Black experience. Ten of the 24 school systems provided for Black Studies as
a separate program. The majority of these programs consisted primarily of a course in Black history. 2. There were 63 high schools
in the state with Black Studies. Most of the programs were initiated because of student demands; however, there was little evidence of student participation in planning and program design. 3.
Few systems had developed their own curriculum guides, and while
flexibility is desirable in content, methods and materials, the
programs appeared excessively variant in these elements, both
among school systems and within school systems. 4. The data studied indicated an apparent need to improve both the selection process and training process of teachers for the program. 5. There
was no evidence in the state of any type of formal evaluation of
the elective Black Studies program. 6. The findings in Prince
Georges County supported the following: (a) the majority of the
individuals in the program were Black, middle class students pre-
paring for college; (b) the program content stressed contemporary
problems and history; and (c) the principals, teachers, and students gave a better than average overall evaluation of the program.

200. Matthews, Robert L. "Black Studies, Academic Achievement and The
Self-Concept of Selected Tenth Graders." Unpublished Doctoral
Dissertation, United States International University, 1971.
121 pp.

The objective of this study was to determine whether certain kinds
of changes would occur in tenth graders enrolled in a "Black Studies" program. Specifically, the aim of the study was to learn
whether participation in "Black Studies" would strengthen the self-
concept, personal development, and academic achievements of Black
youths. Special attention was given to the evaluation that the
enrollees gave to the program. Dr. Matthews made the following
conclusions: (1) On the standardized tests of educational achievement, both groups made appreciable gains, but the gains were not
significantly different; (2) With regard to grade point average,
the data proved not suitable as a rating of performance on change
in academic accomplishments; (3) Although there were no statistically significant differences between the Black Studies students
and the control students, higher grade point averages and fewer
failure grades were recorded for Black Studies students; (4) The

students' favorable evaluation of the Black Studies program as given in interviews contained considerable content that suggest not only valued knowledge which they gained, but improved attitudes toward self and toward others - inclusive of persons of other color.

201. McBride, Ullyssee. "A Survey of Black Studies Offerings in Traditionally Black Institutions of Higher Education Between 1960-73." Unpublished Doctoral Dissertation, Auburn University, 1974. 132 pp.

This study was prompted by the need to examine the Black Studies programs in traditionally Black colleges and universities of higher education in the United States, because of pressures to adopt Black Studies programs in the 1960's. To accomplish this examination, a questionnaire, a variety of materials and personal visits by the researcher were relied upon for information. The most significant findings from the analysis and interpretation of the data were: 1. Black Studies courses were widespread. There were 94.6 percent of the institutions in the study offering courses. 2. Enrollments showed a spectacular decline in the early 1970's. 3. Enrollments included a sprinkling of non-Blacks. 4. Instructors were Black with a sprinkling of non-Blacks. 5. Black institutions adopted Black Studies programs since 1960 (66.22 percent). 6. Regular faculty members taught Black Studies. 7. There were 13 percent of the institutions in the study offering some kind of major in Black Studies. 8. Black students pressed Black institutions to offer Black studies. 9. Graduates with degrees in Black Studies were very few. 10. Afro-American was favored over Black in course titles. 11. Black Studies showed a definite decline, concludes Dr. McBride.

202. Moone, James C. "The Problem of Designing an African-American Studies Program in U.S. Public Schools: The Challenge for New Directions. A Case Study of the Washington, D.C. Public Schools, 1969-1974." Unpublished Doctoral Dissertation, Howard University, 1976. 330 pp.

The writer has attempted to examine the circumstances under which African-Americans have developed a negative concept of self, and searches for ways that Black youth attending Public Schools may develop positive images about Africa, and finally, how this most vital academic area has struggled to maintain its existence from the early 1960's to the present. Chapter I, served as an introduction to the study, Chapter II has to do with the Black Experience: A Historical Background. The various aspects of slavery and its sad dehumanizing of African-Americans are treated in this chapter. Chapter III deals with the Emergence of African-American Studies in Washington, D.C. Public Schools. It also points out the 92 years of segregation, arrival of integration in the mid-1950's and the cause for decline of Black scholarship as well as early efforts to seek Black Studies Program in the Public School System. Chapter IV, National Debate on the Issues Involved in Black Studies Programs, describes the plight of Black Studies programs and specific legislation taken by states and school boards to implement

Black Studies. Chapter V describes Black Studies in Washington,
D.C. School System and points out that the school system is lacking in positive goals for African-American Studies programs.
Chapter VI has to do with <u>Performance and Evaluation of African-
American Studies in D.C. Public Schools</u>. Chapter VII is the Con-
clusion and Recommendation of the study. In this chapter an effort is made to give the essential highlights of the research and
recommendations are made which may be utilized for program development and implementation of African-American Studies in U.S.
Public Schools. It is crucial that school systems do not return
to their former status, therefore, a challenge for "new directions"
is offered by Dr. Moone.

203. Morehead, Qumare A. "A Study of Black Studies in the Social
     Sciences and Humanities Curricula of Ten Colleges and Universities
     in Arkansas." Unpublished Doctoral Dissertation, Kansas State
     University, 1977. 256 pp.

     The purpose of this study was to investigate the status of Black
     Studies in the social sciences and humanities curricula in ten in-
     stitutions of higher education in Arkansas. The study specifically
     attempted to discover perceptions of chairpersons of Social Scien-
     ces and Humanities Departments toward Black Studies, determine the
     number, form and substance of Black Studies courses offered, the
     extent of required Black experience related courses, and the re-
     cency and rationale for including Black Studies in the curriculum
     of the Social Sciences and Humanities Departments. Dr. Morehead
     concludes: (1) Each college and university surveyed in this study
     offers at least one or more courses in Black Studies; to this ex-
     tent it was argued that each institution is playing an active role
     in promoting Black Studies. (2) Respondents overwhelmingly agreed
     that Black Studies is a creative response to the frustrations that
     beset Black Americans, a vehicle for improving relations among the
     races, academically viable, and would benefit students training
     for careers as teachers. (3) Approximately eight-tenths of the
     chairpersons felt that reorganizing traditional courses to include
     achievements and contributions of Blacks is the form Black Studies
     should take on their respective campuses. (4) Of a total of sixty-
     two Black Studies courses listed by the respondents, an overwhelm-
     ing majority of the courses listed were in the sociology, English,
     history and political science departments. (5) The form and sub-
     stance of Black Studies in the institutions consist mainly of vi-
     siting Black lecturers and Afro-American history, literature and
     political science courses. The majority of Black Studies courses
     were offered at the junior and senior levels. (6) More than eight-
     tenths of the Black Studies courses were added to the curriculum
     after 1965. (7) The number of required courses is minimal and
     plans for requiring majors to take Black Studies courses are also
     minimal.

204. Newton, James E. "A Curriculum Evaluation of Black Studies in Re-
     lation to Student Knowledge of Afro-American History and Culture."
     Unpublished Doctoral Dissertation, Illinois State University, 1972.
     158 pp.

The major purpose of the investigation was to evaluate Black Studies in relation to student knowledge of Afro-American history and culture. The purpose was also to provide a description of student attitude toward Black Studies programs. It was necessary to develop and utilize an instrument to measure student knowledge of Afro-American culture. The general hypothesis for this investigation is that students in Black Studies Curriculum will be more familiar with Afro-Americans and their contributions to society and will have more positive attitudes toward Black Studies. Dr. Newton concludes: "The statistical evaluation indicated that the Black Studies curriculum Group tends to be more familiar with knowledge of Afro-American history and culture and is better able to identify specific Afro-American personalities. Students in the Black Studies Curriculum Group also indicated a higher significance in attitude towards studies about Afro-Americans."

205. Palcic, James L. "The History of the Black Student Union at Florida State University." Unpublished Doctoral Dissertation, Florida State University, 1979. 376 pp.

The objective of this study was to develop a history of the Black Student Union at Florida State University from the founding of the organization in the Spring of 1968 through June, 1978. The findings indicated that the formation of the Black Student Union was a reaction to the feelings of alienation and ostracism of Black students on the predominantly white campus of Florida State University. The organization emerged from the desire of Black students to enter the mainstream of campus life and to challenge institutional racism. During the period from April, 1968, when the organization was founded, through June, 1972, the Black Student Union presented proposals, resolutions and demands to the administration. This student group initiated the development of Black Studies courses, the Office of Minority Student Affairs, and the Black Students' Educational and Cultural Center. The Black Student Union became a political force within the student culture and elected members to offices in university-wide elections. The group also became the major producer of Black-oriented entertainment, lectures, and art on the FSU campus. While there were confrontations between the Black Student Union and Student Government over funds, the principal adversary of the Black Student Union from 1968 to 1972 was found to be Florida State University administration. After June, 1972 the number of confrontations between the Black Student Union and Florida State University decreased. This investigator found that the principal adversary of the organization during this later period was the Student Government. The Black Student Union was successful in initiating an interdisciplinary academic program in Afro-American Studies and a Black Studies minor. The group also became more involved in campus politics by forming coalitions with other predominantly white student organizations that were supportive of the goals of the Black Student Union, concludes the writer.

206. Parker, Margaret B. "Black Studies in the Community Colleges of New Jersey: A Topographical Study." Unpublished Doctoral Dissertation, Rutgers University, 1976. 213 pp.

The purpose of this study was to establish a topography, or detailed summation of Black Studies in the community colleges of New Jersey. An examination of the nomothetic, ideographic and cultural dimensions of such courses was made in constructing the topography. This study also sought to ascertain if generalizations could be formulated in regard to the extent to which Black Studies in the community colleges in New Jersey was influenced by the urban or suburban nature of the counties within which they existed, the constituencies which they served or the chronology of their establishment between 1966 and 1975. The topography summarized the number of full-time Black faculty, or professional staff, administrators and trustees at each college; the number of Blacks on Advisory Boards, the number of Black Studies courses and Black student organizations, and the number of Blacks in the student population of the college as well as in the counties which these colleges serve. It was argued that the urban or suburban nature of the community colleges studied did not appreciably influence the presence or absence of Black Studies courses, as they were found in all colleges. The chronology of their establishment and the constituencies which they serve were ascertained to have influenced the presence or absence of Black Studies courses, concludes the author.

207. Polk, Travis R. "The Status of the Teaching of Negro History in the Public High Schools of Texas." Unpublished Doctoral Dissertation, North Texas State University, 1972. 149 pp.

This study is concerned with the status of the teaching of Negro history in American history classes in the public high schools of Texas. Efforts were made to obtain information relative to the (1) organization of Negro history for instruction, (2) objectives teachers consider most important in teaching Negro history, (3) kind and extent of preparation for teaching Negro history, (4) evaluative procedures employed by teachers, (5) instructional materials and methods which teachers used most extensively, and (6) the extent of opposition to teaching Negro history as perceived by teachers. The author came to the following conclusions: (1) A majority of the American history teachers in the public high schools of Texas believe that Negro history is a significant part of American history and that Negro history is beneficial to their Caucasian as well as their Negro students. (2) A majority of the American history teachers believe that teaching Negro history will help reduce interracial tensions and that the Negro child's self-concept would be improved through a study of his heritage. (3) A majority of the American history teachers believe that Negro history should be integrated into the American history course, rather than being taught as a separate, elective course. (4) A majority of the American history teachers consider the development of an understanding of the intercultural responsibilities of American citizens to be the most significant objective in teaching Negro history. (5) A majority of the American history teachers lack sufficient preparation for teaching the role of the Negro in American history. (6) More of the American history teachers in larger metropolitan areas tend to be more concerned with teaching Negro history than do American history teachers in the smaller communities or rural areas.

208. Rhinehart, Charles P. "Effecting Attitude Change Through Music Presented By An Integrative Black Studies Approach." Unpublished Doctoral Dissertation, University of Houston, 1972. 267 pp.

The central concern of the study was to determine the nature of changes in attitudes of students completing a one-semester introductory music course in which the Black artistic dimension had been structurally integrated by merging with existing course contents the contributions of Black musicians. Followiing an extended review of the development of the role of Black Studies, attitudes as a function of ethnic perceptions, and expanding esthetic experiences through music, a course was structured which would implement the Black dimension as a pedagogical device. The writer concludes: "Concerning attitude toward aesthetics, the control group showed no change from pretest to posttest, while experimental group showed positive change. Analysis of data indicated the Black dimension had even greater impact for positive attitude toward the introductory course in music than for aesthetics generally. Undoubtedly the experimental subjects considered the course as having relevance and meaning for them and they were enabled to see the black man's role in fine arts in an enlightened perspective. Positive change was found for control subjects." Dr. Rhinehart recommended that parallel research using a Black Studies approach be carried out in other areas of the fine arts and in the social sciences. It was concluded that through the process of attitudinal alteration and its implication for the entire educational system that similar or related projects have potential far beyond the present investigation.

209. Simms, Ruby J. "The Effects of Black Studies' Instruction on The Self-Concept of Senior High School Students." Unpublished Doctoral Dissertation, The Louisiana State University and Agricultural and Mechanical College, 1976. 170 pp.

Three supplementary units dealing with the Black experience prior to the Civil War were constructed by the researcher and taught by three of the regularly assigned male students (one Black and two whites) to Black senior high school students. The purpose of this study was to investigate the effects of such instruction on the self-concepts of the students. The author found no statistically significant differences between the self-concept scores for the experimental and control group students in the areas of Self-Criticism; Identity; Self-Satisfaction; Physical Self; Personal Self; and Social Self. "T"-values were to the left of the assumed mean difference of zero, for the two groups in the areas of Behavior; Family Self; and total Positive Scores. Since the .05 level of confidence was not reached, the first full null hypothesis was accepted, states Dr. Simms. The analysis of the data indicated a

statistically significant difference was obtained between the com-
bined groups and male students only under one category - Moral-
Ethical Self. However, trends toward change in self-concept were
observed in several other categories, concludes the author.

210. Simson, Renate M. "A Survey Analysis of Some Issues Related to
     Content and Effectiveness of Black Literature Courses Taught in
     Colleges and Universities in New York State." Unpublished Doctoral
     Dissertation, Syracuse University, 1974. 233 pp.

A great deal has been written theorizing about Black Studies courses, but surprisingly few studies have been undertaken to examine
the relationship between theory and practice. This survey was
undertaken to explore certain aspects of Black Literature courses
about which much theorizing, but little objective investigation
has been done. Dr. Simson states that the majority of students indicated that taking a Black Literature course had been a positive
experience for them. White students reported a considerable increase in their understanding of the Black experience and their
respect for the intellectual achievement of Blacks. Blacks did
not report great increases in self-confidence or ethnic confidence,
but many reported they had always had such confidence. Members of
neither race reported that the course had helped them to improve
their relations with members of the other race. Approximately one-
third of the students reported that the course increased their sym-
pathy with demonstrations by Blacks, both peaceful and violent.
Dr. Simson concludes: "Taking a Black Literature course definitely produced changes in outlook in a sizable number of students."

211. Smith, Glenn R. "The Black Studies Program At The University of
     Colorado (Boulder and Denver Campuses) 1968-1973: Development,
     Change and Assessments" Unpublished Doctoral Dissertation, Univer-
     sity of Colorado, 1974. 133 pp.

The purpose of this study is to examine the development of the
Black Studies Program at the University of Colorado (Boulder and
Denver campuses) with respect to change agents and change methodologies, and to assess this Program as the stated objectives.
Major findings of the study include: 1. The number of courses offered through the Black Studies Program has increased on both campuses. 2. The number of personnel under contract specifically for
the Black Studies Program has increased on the Boulder and Denver
campuses. 3. The number of students enrolled in the Black Studies
Program has increased on both campuses. 4. There has been a substantial increase in the general fund allocations to the Black
Studies Program on the Boulder campus, while there has been no significant increase in allocations for the program on the Denver campus. 5. The Black experience had not been exposed to the University students. 6. The short-range objectives of the programs were
consistent with need assessment as defined by the Jessor Report.
7. The long-range objectives of the programs are not consistent
with need assessment. 8. There was no formal planning or organization prior to the implementation of the programs. 9. The programs were inadequately staffed, no office facilities were offered

to the programs. Funds for the operation of the programs were drawn from the general budget and were inadequate, according to both directors. 10. No systematic observations or monitoring of program activities exists. Information or feedback is inadequate for the measurements of the Black Studies programs in achieving their major objectives.

212. Sutton, William S. "The Evolution of the Black Studies Movement: With Specific Reference to the Establishment of the Black Studies Institute at Ohio University." Unpublished Doctoral Dissertation, Ohio University, 1972. 342 pp.

This investigation outlines the establishment of the Black Studies Institute at Ohio University which followed the same stages of development as those in other predominantly white institutions. These stages are: 1. an exploratory or deliberative stage in which a Black Organization is formed to outline the form and content of a Black Studies program; 2. a rallying of the forces stage which is characterized by the Black Student organization seeking support for its program by uniting with larger Black student population on the campus to create the illusion of total Black unity; 3. a confrontation stage in which demands for a Black Studies program are presented to university officials; 4. a concession or conciliation stage in which the institution waives its usual requirements and standards to accommodate the demands of the Black students and; 5. a stage of institutionalization in which Black Studies program becomes a part of the institution proper. Underlying these stages is a thrust toward Black nationalism using the campus and Black Studies programs as a strategy toward achieving a quasi-form of Black nationalism in America.

213. Taylor, Hurl R., Jr. "Effects of Black Studies Training and Human Relations Training On the Attitudes of Graduate Students In Education." Unpublished Doctoral Dissertation, Georgia State University, 1974. 183 pp.

The study was undertaken to determine the effects of a combination of Black studies and human relations training on the attitudes of graduate students in education. The problems experienced in the desegregation and integration of educational institutions across the nation followed by racial unrest in society in general during the transitional period provided the initial stimulus and motivation for the study. The study was focused around four general areas: (a) change in cognitive knowledge; (b) Black self-awareness; (c) white acceptance, and (d) change in attitudes. Dr. Taylor found the following results: 1. Cognitive knowledge of Black culture increased. 2. Black self-awareness did not increase. 3. There was limited evidence to indicate that white subjects increased their acceptance of the Black's quest for equality. 4. There was limited evidence to indicate that all subjects changed their racial attitudes in a favorable manner. 5. There was limited evidence to indicate that change in racial attitudes occurred after human relations training and not Black studies training. 6. The order of training in Black studies and human relations did not influence either change in cognitive knowledge or racial attitude.

214. Vargus, Ione D. "Revival of Ideology: The Afro-American Society Movement." Unpublished Doctoral Dissertation, Brandeis University, 1971. 207 pp.

Dr. Vargus concludes that on the issue of Black studies, the emphasis has evolved from the demand for a few courses on Black history and culture to the creation of a "Black University." Although on the issues of Black facilities, there is a mixed stance regarding the strategy of demanding all-Black dormitories, there is general agreement on the need for a Black Cultural Center. Furthermore, on the issue of recruitment of students and faculty, the central concern, above and beyond the increase of both, is that of qualifications which differ from the traditional guidelines used in practices of admissions and hiring. Dr. Vargus concludes: "The Afro-American Societies are also communicators of the ideologies circulating in the larger Black society. They present "cultural" weekends that are essentially educational and political in nature; they publish their own papers which are for Black audiences, and distribute these across the country."

215. Wallace, Joan Edaire S. "Afro-American Studies in a Suburban Woman's College: A Case Study." Unpublished Doctoral Dissertation, Northwestern University, 1973. 221 pp.

This work focused on the evolutionary process of an Afro-American Studies program, its history, implementation and first year impacts on an upper middle class (white) suburban women's college. Dr. Wallace concludes: (1) Black students want in - not out of the American mainstream. (2) Afro-American Studies courses are seen as incremental rather than a substitute for regular courses. (3) Black students experience isolation in various degrees on white campuses. (4) White students in Black Studies courses exhibit behaviors similar to those attributed to Black students in regular courses. (5) White students who take Black Studies courses have higher internal control scores that white students not taking the courses. (6) White registrants in Black Studies courses experience a decrease in their attitudes regarding the control of their fate. (7) Afro-American Studies courses are perceived by white faculty as easier than traditional offerings. (8) Both Black and white students expect Black faculty to be easier than white faculty. (9) A multi-faceted Afro-American Studies program which includes counseling is more effective in meeting the needs of Black students on white campuses.

216. Wheeler, Barbara Anne. "Curriculum Development in Higher Education: Black Nationalism, Black Student Protest and Black Studies." Unpublished Doctoral Dissertation, Columbia University Teachers College, 1980. 343 pp.

Prompted by the need to understand the confusion and conflict which attended the introduction of Black Studies into the university curriculum, this dissertation attempts to examine the historical and political origins of the demand for this controversial educational innovation. Observation and a rather superficial knowledge of the historical record led to the initial hypothesis which further

investigation of the literature appeared to support. Concisely
stated, the demand for Black Studies could be viewed as the logical outgrowth of the intersection of at least three historical
movements which collided in time and space and produced the vortex
which swept the demand for organized knowledge about the Black experience onto the social consciousness and the university campus,
suggests the author. The value of this dissertation resides in
the organization and presentation of accessible, but unharnessed
data which demonstrate the historical continuity of the Black protest activities which resulted in the demand for Black Studies.
A significant by-product of the endeavor has been the development
of a curriculum, which, in its present or an altered form, may
prove useful for Black Studies courses, states Dr. Wheeler. The
need for such an extensive presentation resides primarily in the
assumption that knowledge facilitates understanding and that understanding will help to assure the retention of Black Studies as
an area of academic inquiry, concludes the writer.

217. White, Milo Ritter. "The Teaching of the History of the Negro in
Selected Secondary Schools in Michigan." Unpublished Doctoral
Dissertation, University of Michigan, 1970. 268 pp.

This investigation explored the teaching of Negro history in
grades 10 through 12 in selected Michigan secondary schools. In
May and June, 1969, a sample of fifty-two teachers and administrators in forty-three schools with varying percentages of Negro and
white students was interviewed concerning the teaching of Negro
history. Three different courses were identified: (1) the separate course, an elective concerned primarily with Negro history;
(2) the integrative course, the regular American history course
which recently included content and materials on Negro history;
(3) the traditional course, the regular course with no additional
content on the Negro beyond that presented in the typical history
textbook. Dr. White concludes: "The Negro student in the separate courses was perceived to have improved his academic performance substantially and to have experienced a change in his attitudes toward self, the white majority, and the civil rights movement. There was no substantial opposition to the adoption and the
diffusion of the separate and the integrative courses attributable
to the properties of these courses or to the characteristics of
the educational system. Changes in the Negro student's attitudes
were perceived by respondents, but extensive reforms in the educational environment were judged necessary for these changes to be
meaningful."

218. Williams, Clarence G. "An Investigation of the Basic 'Affective
Dimensions' of the Black Tradition and of Black Studies in Higher
Education." Unpublished Doctoral Dissertation, University of
Connecticut, 1971. 114 pp.

This dissertation states that it is feasible to develop an instrument that will differentiate among and assess the degree of acceptance of certain selected concepts related to the Black tradition
in colleges and universities. However, as an on-going development

of this instrument, additional empirical investigation relative to
underlying relationships between factors and their reliabilities
should be undertaken.   Stated Dr. Williams: This study sampled
135 undergraduates and 23 graduate students at the University of
Connecticut at Starrs.

219. Williams, Willie Lee.   "Curriculum for Teaching the Black Experience Through Music and Dramatic History."   Unpublished Doctoral
Dissertation, University of Massachusetts, 1972.   136 pp.

During the past two decades, the plea from Black students and the
community has been to obtain an effective Black Studies program.
These voices have spread to the colleges, universities, and the
public schools.   Their plea has led many administrators and teachers to implement some form of a Black Studies program.   This
study and proposed curriculum guide is to show the reader that
students can be more honest about their feelings and their com-
plexities, and recognize that their responses and attitudes when
confronted by the facts of race are a peculiar combination of the
particular and the general.   Their attitudes are uniquely theirs,
but they are very like the humorous responses of others.   In view
of ever-changing curriculums and relevance of racial attitudes
throughout the country, this study is based upon experimentation
in the Springfield School System in Springfield, Massachusetts, in
1971 and 1972.   However, it is proposed that it can be implemented
in any school system seeking innovative education, concludes Dr.
Williams.

220. Wilson, Henry, Jr.   "A Descriptive Study of Selected Black Studies
Units in American Colleges and Universities."   Unpublished Doctoral Dissertation, Southern Illinois University, 1972.   204 pp.

This investigation was focused on the analysis and interpretation
of data from twenty "successful" college and university Black
Studies units.   The focus of the data was on the areas of origin
and organization, objectives and mission, curriculum, faculty,
students, service and administration.   Major findings were that
these "successful" Black Studies units were characterized by
"borrowed" courses and shared faculty and facilities; that the
administrative heads of these units perceive student support to be
weak, in spite of considerable student involvement in top level
decision-making, and white faculty to be opposed; that units apparently used considerable resources for services primarily to
the off-campus Black community; that the overall support of these
units as given by the on-campus and the off-campus communities as
perceived by the unit heads is unenthusiastic; and that the financial support given these units was generally static, showing signs
of decrease.   This investigation attempted to describe what appears
to have developed over a period of less than five years in a rela-
tively new field of area studies.   Dr. Wilson concludes: "Looking
at the history of curricular reform in institutions of American
higher education, it is not entirely clear what this recent innovation of Black Studies means.   Presently it may be only safe to
say that Black Studies in American colleges and universities is in-
dicative of a student-generated renewal of interest in the Black
experience in the American academic community."

221. Wilson, Roselle L. "Case Studies of Institutionalization: Black
     Ethnic Studies and Other Interdisciplinary Curricula." Unpublish-
     ed Doctoral Dissertation, University of Michigan, 1978. 394 pp.

     This is a study of the institutionalization of interdisciplinary
     curricula in higher education, particularly Black Studies. The
     findings highlight the institutionalization of Black/Ethnic Stu-
     dies in four institutions of higher education. Institutions
     which anticipated Black Studies Programs had faculty and adminis-
     trators who were able to implement, support, and continue the
     commitment to their development. Institutions which responded to
     the demands of student activities in the sixties reached the point
     of implementing but not institutionalizing a Black/Ethnic Studies
     program. Faculty and administrators in these institutions have
     some difficulty continuing support for a Black/Ethnic Studies pro-
     gram. Dr. Wilson states that in each case administrators were
     found to be more supportive of Black/Ethnic Studies than faculty
     members. Administrators in the less accepting institutions were
     moderately concerned about the issues surrounding Black/Ethnic
     Studies. The faculty who were most supportive were in departments
     that were closely involved with either teaching Black/Ethnic Stu-
     dies, offering joint appointments to Black Studies faculty, or
     working in an advisory role to Black/Ethnic Studies programs.
     Another finding of this study was that comparable interdisciplina-
     ry programs and Black/Ethnic Studies programs had very different
     beginnings, but as they entered the formal university curriculum
     structure they had similar problems and obstacles. They seemed to
     converge at a point following the implementation stage, concludes
     Dr. Wilson.

222. Zunino, Gerald J. "An Examination of American Negro - Afro-Ameri-
     can History and Its Relationship to the Senior High School Social
     Studies Curriculum." Unpublished Doctoral Dissertation, Univer-
     sity of Southern California, 1971. 508 pp.

     The purpose of the study was to determine the extent of agreement
     or disagreement among historians and educators as to the purposes
     and methodology for writing and teaching American Negro history as
     well as the facts and interpretations which it should include. Ad-
     ditionally, the intent was to determine whether recently developed
     senior high school curricula in this area were historically accu-
     rate in light of recent scholarship. Dr. Zunino concluded: (1)
     Historians and educators disagreed as to the purpose, content, in-
     terpretation and methodology of American Negro history courses.
     For example, some favored courses that would objectively discuss
     the historical roles of both whites and Blacks and would be taught
     by persons of any race. Others favored courses that would enhance
     Black pride and promote Black Nationalism and would be taught pri-
     marily by Blacks; (2) Historians disagreed as to interpretations
     of certain areas of American Negro history; (3) Curricula currently
     used varied widely as to format and as to the grade levels and
     types of courses for which they were intended; (4) The curricula
     were in partial agreement with recent historical scholarship.
     While almost all contained some results of recent research, few
     were considered consistently adequate throughout. The most obvious

deficiencies were the omission or inadequate explanation of certain significant topics. Another serious deficiency was the frequent absence of explanations of historiographical techniques as well as the existence of, reasons for, and results of disagreements among historians, argues Prof. Zunino.

4.
ARTICLES

A Selected List*

223.*ABD-AL Hakimu Ibn Alkalimat (Gerald McWorter), "The Ideology of Black Social Science", Black Scholar, Vol. 1, No. 4, December, 1969, pp. 28-35.

224. Abromowitz, Jack. "Textbooks and Negro History", Social Education, Vol. 33, No. 3, March, 1969, pp. 306-309.

225. Adams, Russell L. "Black Studies Perspectives", Journal of Negro Education, Vol. 46, No. 2, Spring, 1977, pp. 114-117.

226.*_____. "Evaluating Professionalism in the Context of Afro-American Studies", Western Journal of Black Studies, Vol. 4, No. 2, Summer, 1980, pp. 140-148.

227.*Adams, William E. "Black Studies in Elementary Schools", Journal of Negro Education, Vol 39, No. 3, Summer, 1970, pp. 202-209.

228. "Afro-American Research Unit for Harvard", Negro History Bulletin, Vol. 33, No. 7, November 1970, p. 170.

229. "Afro-American Studies Program at the University of Houston", Brochure (University of Houston), 1971.

230. "Afro-American Study Programs: Curriculum of Michigan Catholic School System", America, Vol. 119, November 23, 1968, p. 508.

231. "Agony at State: Problems of San Francisco State College", Newsweek, Vo. 71, No. 4, January 22, 1968, p. 59.

232. Allen, Robert L. "Politics of the Attack on Black Studies", Black Scholar, Vol. 6, No. 1, September, 1974, pp. 2-7.

233. Alsop, Joseph. "'Black Studies' Drive Faces Tests of Its Academic Validity", Washington Post, February 17, 1969, p. A-12.

*Denotes major article.

234. Aptheker, Herbert. "Black Studies and United States History", Negro History Bulletin, Vol. 34, No. 8, December, 1971, pp. 174-175.

235.* _____. "Black Studies and United States History", Journal of Negro History, Vol. 56, No. 1, January, 1972, pp. 99-105.

236. "As Guns Are Added to Campus Revolts: Cornell University Surrenders to Negroes' Demands", U.S. News & World Report, Vol. 66, No. 18, May 5, 1969, pp. 30-31.

237. Asher, Frank. "Small Price For Black History", Daily World, November 2, 1979, p. 12.

238. Aukema, Richard L. "Oshkosh: Black Student Revolt in Microcosm", Christian Century, Vol. 86, No. 7, February 12, 1969, pp. 219-221.

239. BAILEY, Ronald B. "Opinions Differ on Black Studies: Another Viewpoint", Today's Education, Vol. 62, No. 7, November-December, 1973, pp. 86-88.

240.* _____. "Why Black Studies?" Saint Louis University Magazine, Winter, 1970.

241. Baird, Bernard. "Black Studies Behind New Campus Battlecry", New York Post, March 15, 1969, p. 15.

242 Banks, James A. "Relevant Social Studies for Black Pupils", Social Education, Vol. 33, No. 1, January, 1969, pp. 66-69.

243.* _____. "Teaching Black Studies for Social Change", Journal of Afro-American Issues, Vol. 1, No. 2, Fall, 1971, pp. 141-164.

244. Baraka, Imamu Amiri. "A Reply To Saunders Redding's "The Black Revolution in American Studies", American Studies International, Vol. 17, No. 4, Summer, 1979, pp. 15-24.

245. Baratz, Stephen S. and Joan C. Baratz. "Negro Ghetto Children and Urban Education", Social Education, Vol. 33, No. 4, April, 1969, pp. 401-404.

246. Baren, D. "Do You Date: Negro Literature and the Disadvantaged Student", Phi Delta Kappan, Vol. 50, May, 1969, pp. 520-524.

247. Bass, J. and P. Clancy. "Militant Mood in Negro Colleges", Reporter, Vol. 38, May 16, 1968, pp. 21-23.

248, "Behind Revolt of Black Students", U.S. News & World Report, Vol. 67, No. 12, September 22, 1969, p. 16.

249. Bennett, Lerone. "Confrontation on the Campus", Ebony, Vol. 23, No. 7, May, 1968, pp. 27-30.

250. Berry, L. "The Teaching of Afro-American Music and Black History - An Interdisciplinary Program", College Music Symposium, Vol. 23, No. 1, Spring, 1983, p. 185.

251. Billingsley, Andrew, et al. "Ethnic Studies at Berkeley", Califor-
     nia Monthly, Vol., 8, June-July, 1970, pp. 12-20.

252. "Black and White at Northwestern University", Integrated Education,
     Vol. 6, No. 3, May-June, 1968, pp. 33-48.

253. "Black Dimension in Curriculum", School and Society, Vol. 97, No.
     2315, February, 1969, p. 83.

254. "Black History - As Schools Teach It", U.S. News & World Report,
     Vol. 65, No. 19, November 4, 1968, pp. 68-71.

255. "Black is Beautiful, and Belligerent", Time, Vol. 93, No. 4,
     January 24, 1969, p. 43.

256. "Black is...for Credit", Newsweek, Vol. 74, No. 16, October 20,
     1969, pp. 102-103.

257. "Black Mood on Campus: Symposium", Newsweek, Vol. 73, No. 6,
     February 10, 1969, pp. 53-59.

258. "Black Studies: A Top Negro's (Andrew F. Brimmer) View", U.S. News
     & World Report, Vol. 67, No. 10, September 8, 1969, pp. 12, 34.

259. "Black Studies and The University - Northwestern University",
     Integrated Education, Vol. 7, No. 2, March-April, 1969, pp. 27-33.

260.*"Black Studies and Writing: Symposium", Negro History Bulletin,
     Vol. 36, No. 2, February, 1973, pp. 28-36.

261. "Black Studies Courses Added in Three Departments", Bryn Mawr
     Alumnae Bulletin, Summer, 1969, p. 5.

262. "Black Studies First At Lincoln (PA) University Set", Muhammed
     Speaks, May 16, 1969, p. 1.

263. "Black Studies: Fuse or Pacifier?" America, Vol. 122, No. 22,
     May 23, 1970, pp. 548-549.

264. "Black Studies in the USA Including African Studies", West Africa,
     August 9, 1969, pp. 919, 921.

265. "Black Studies Offered At 250 Colleges", Sacramento (CA) Observer,
     February 12, 1970, p. 24.

266.*"Black Studies: Perspective 1970", Danforth (Foundation) News and
     Notes, Vol. 5, No. 2, March, 1970, pp. 1-4.

267. "Black Studies Pose Quandary", Washington Post, March 16, 1969,
     pp. B-1, B-2, B-3.

268. "Black Studies Program at SUNY at Buffalo Appears Questionable",
     Reporter, (SUNY at Buffalo), February 12, 1976, p. 8.

269. "Black Studies Programs", Educational Digest, Vol. 24, No. 8,
     April 1969, p. 60.

270. "Black Studies Rallies For Its Survival", Encore: American and Worldwide News, Vol. 6, No. 3, March 21, 1977, p. 14.

271. "Black Studies Runs Into Trouble on U.S. College Campuses", U.S. News & World Report, Vol. 74, No. 5, January 29, 1973, pp. 29-32.

272. "Black Studies Studied: American Council on Education Report", America, June 21, 1969, p. 698.

273. "Black Studies Succeed", Air Force Times, Vol. 31, April 28, 1971, p. 20.

274. "Black Studies Takeover Sought", Afro-American, April 7, 1970.

275. "Black Studies To Begin At Maryland U.", Washington Sunday Star, August 3, 1969, p. A-1.

276. "Black Studies: Yes or No?" America, May 17, 1969, pp. 578-579.

277. Blake, Cecil A. "Critical Issues in Black Studies: Edward Blyden's Rhetoric on Black Education", Western Journal of Black Studies, Vol. 2, No. 2, Summer, 1978, pp. 157-160.

278.*Blassingame, John W. "Black Studies: An Intellectual Crisis", American Scholar, Vol. 38, No. 4, 1969, pp. 548-561.

279.*_____. "Soul or Scholarship: An Examination of Black Studies So Far What Students Learn About History", Smithsonian, Vol. 1, No. 1, April, 1970, pp. 58-64.

280. Bode, Elroy. "El Paso Dialogue: The Rhetoric of Revenge: First Black Student Conference in the Southwest", Nation, Vol. 206, No. 18, April 29, 1968, pp. 58-64.

281.*Bolden, Otis L. "The Educational Institutions: A Crucible For Black Identity", Journal of Afro-American Issues, Vol. 2, No. 4, Fall, 1974, pp. 348-360.

282. Bornhold, Laura. "Black Studies: Perspective, 1971", Danforth (Foundation) News and Notes, Vol. 6, No. 2, March, 1971, p. 1.

283. Boskin, Joseph. "Black Identity and Black Studies", Los Angeles Times, December 12, 1968.

284. Boutwell, W. D. "Teaching the History of the Negro", PTA Journal, Vol. 62, No. 3, March 1968, p. 15.

285.*Bracey, John. "Black Studies Tenure and Promotion: A Reply to Davidson", Review of Black Political Economy, Vol. 10, No. 3, Spring, 1980, pp. 375-382.

286. Brichman, William W. "The Black Studies Bandwagon", School and Society, Vol. 98, No. 3, March, 1970, p. 140.

287. Brown, Herman. "Black Studies at Predominantly Black Colleges and Universities", Negro History Bulletin, Vol. 36, No. 2, February, 1973, pp. 34-36.

288. Brown, Letitia W. "Why and How the Negro in History", Journal of Negro Education, Vol. 38, No. 4, Spring, 1969, pp. 447-452.

289. Brown, Roscoe C., Jr. "New York University: The Institute of Afro-American Affairs", Journal of Negro Education, Vol. 39, No. 3, Summer, 1970, pp. 214-220.

290.*Browne, Robert S. "The Challenge of Black Student Organization", Freedomways, Vol. 8, No. 4, Fall, 1968, pp. 325-333.

291. Brudnoy, David. "Doves vs. Hawks on Campus: Brandeis", National Review, Vol. 21, No. 7, February 25, 1969, pp. 172-174.

292. _____. "Report From Brandeis University" The Black Power Play", National Review, Vol. 21, No. 3, January 28, 1969, p. 66.

293. Buchanan, Robert. "The Fervor For Black Studies Has Cooled", Washington Sunday Star, October 8, 1972, pp. E-1, E-4.

294.*Bulter, Johnnella E. "Black Studies and Sensibility: Identity, The Foundation For a Pedagogy", Western Journal of Black Studies, Vol. 3, No. 4, Winter, 1979, pp. 290-293.

295. Bunzel, John H. "An Arrogant Minority Victimized the College", Look, Vol. 33, No. 11, May 27, 1969, pp. 62, 70, 72.

296.* _____. "Black Studies at San Francisco State", Public Interest, Vol. 13, Fall, 1968, pp. 22-28.

297. Burns, David. "Museum With a Mission: A Role in Black Studies", Africa Report, Vol. 14, Nos. 5-6, May-June, 1969, pp. 30-33.

298. "CAMPUS Spring Offensive", Newsweek, Vol. 73, No. 17, April 28, 1969, pp. 67-68.

299. "Campus Unrest: New Forces Meets Forces", U.S. News & World Report, Vol. 66, No. 8, February 24, 1969, pp. 8-9.

300.*Carey, Philip and Donald Allen. "Black Studies: Expectation and Impact on Self-Esteem and Academic Performance", Social Science Quarterly, Vol. 57, No. 4, March, 1977, pp. 811-820.

301. Carter, Luther J. "University of Michigan: Black Activists Win a Change of Priorities", Science, Vol. 168, No. 3928, April 10, 1970, pp. 229-231.

302. "Can the University Survive the Black Challenge", Saturday Review, Vol. 52, No. 25, June 21, 1969, pp. 68-71.

303. Cassese, Sid, "LI's Black History Unfolds in Talk", Long Island (NY) Newsday, February 24, 1981.

304. Chapman, William. "Duke University Assents to Demands by Negroes", Washington Post, February 17, 1969, pp. A-1, A-2.

305. Cheek, King V., Jr. "Black Students, Black Studies, Black Col-
     leges", Chronicle of Higher Education, Vol. 6, No. 9, November 22,
     1971, p. 8.

306. Chew, Peter. "Black History or Black Mythology?" American Heri-
     tage, Vol. 20, No. 5, August 1969, pp. 4-9, 104-106.

307. Childs, Charles. "Black Studies at Cornell: The Troubled Path to
     Understanding", Life, Vol. 68, No. 14, April 17, 1970, pp. 56-60.

308. _____. "Gun Comes to Cornell", Life, Vol. 66, No. 17, May 2,
     1969, pp. 20-27.

309. Chinweizu. "Education for Power", First World, Vol. 1, No. 3,
     May/June, 1977, pp. 20-24.

310. Clark, Kenneth B. "A Charade of Power: Students at White Colleges",
     Antioch Review, Vol. 29, No. 2, Summer 1969, pp. 145-148.

311.*Clarke, Anthony. "Ethnic Studies: Reflection and Re-Examination",
     Journal of Negro Education, Vol. 46, No. 2, Spring, 1977, pp. 124-
     132.

312. Clarke, Austin C. "Cultural-Political Origins of Black Student
     Anti-Intellectualism", Studies in Black Literature, Vol. 1, Spring,
     1970, pp. 69-82.

313.*Clarke, John Henrik. "African-American Historians and the Re-
     claiming of African History", Journal of African Studies, Vol. 7,
     No. 2, Summer, 1980, pp. 91-98.

314.*_____. "The Fight to Reclaim African History", Negro Digest,
     Vol. 19, No. 2, February, 1970, pp. 10-15.

315. Cleaver, Eldridge. "Education and Revolution", Black Scholar,
     Vol. 1, No. 1, November, 1969, pp. 44-52.

316. Clements, Clyde C., Jr., "Black Studies for White Students",
     Negro American Literature Forum, Vol. 4, No. 1, March, 1970,
     pp. 9-11.

317. Cleveland, B. "Black Studies and Higher Education", Phi Delta
     Kappan, Vol. 51, September, 1969, pp. 44-46.

318. Cochell, Shirley. "Discovering the Negro's Contributions",
     Catholic School Journal, Vol. 68, 1968, pp. 34-35.

319. Cohen, Richard M. "U.S. Takes Action to Desegregate Black Studies:
     Antioch Faces Loss of Funds", Washington Post, March 6, 1969, pp.
     A-1, A-11.

320. Colen, B.D. "Negro History Courses Prove Popular at (DC Universi-
     ties)", Washington Post, February 9, 1969, p. A-1.

321.*Coles, Flournoy. "Black Studies in the College Curriculum",
     Negro Educational Review, Vol. 20, No. 4, October 1969, pp. 106-113.

322. "College Beset by Black Revolutionaries: Federal City College, Washington, DC", U.S. News & World Report, Vol. 66, No. 19, May 12, 1969, pp. 38-40.

323. Colon, Alan K. "Black Studies: What Divisiveness?" Washington Post, December 13, 1982, p. A-14.

324. Colquit, Jesse L. "The Teacher's Dilemma in Facilitating the Black Experience", Journal of Negro Education, Vol. 47, No. 2, Spring, 1978, pp. 192-200.

325. Colt, George Howe. "Will the (Nathan) Huggins Approach Save Afro-American Studies?" Harvard Magazine, September-October, 1981, pp. 38-46, 62, 70.

326. "Conclusions About Cornell", Time, Vol. 94, No. 12, September 19, 1969, p. 44.

327.*Cook, Samuel Dubois. "A Tragic Conception of Negro History", Journal of Negro History, Vol 45, No. 4, October, 1960, pp. 219-240.

328. "Cornell: The Black Studies Thing", New Times Magazine, April 6, 1969, p. 25.

329. "Cornell U Sets Up Afro-American Studies Program", New York Times, September 15, 1969, p. 18.

330. Cotton, Barbara R. "Teaching Nineteenth Century Afro-American History: The Case Study Approach", Western Journal of Black Studies, Vol. 3, No. 1, Spring, 1979, pp. 72-76.

331. Cottrell, Elaine. "Black Studies", Raleigh Magazine, Vols. 3 & 4, 1971, pp. 34-35.

332. Coyne, John R., Jr. "The Siege of San Francisco State", National Review, Vol. 21, No. 3, January 28, 1969, pp. 67-68.

333.*Crouchett, Lawrence. "Early Black Studies Movements", Journal of Black Studies, Vol. 2, No. 2, December, 1971, pp. 189-200.

334. Crowder, Ralph L. "Historical Significance of Black History Month", Western Journal of Black Studies, Vol. 1, No. 4, December, 1977, pp. 302-304.

335.*Cuban, Larry. "Black History, Negro History, and White Folk", Teaching Social Studies to Culturally Different Children. Reading, MA: Addison-Wesley Publishing Co., 1971.

336. _____. "Black or Negro History", Bulletin of the National Association of Secondary School Principals, Vol. 54, No. 2, 1970, pp. 1-6.

337. _____. "Not 'Whether?' But 'Why' and 'How'?" Journal of Negro Education, Vol. 36, No. 4, Fall, 1967, pp. 434-436.

338. Cudjoe, Selwyn R. "Needed: A Black Studies Consortium", Liberator, Vol. 9, September, 1969, pp. 14-15.

339. *Cummings, Robert. "African and Afro-American Studies Centers: Towards A Cooperative Relationship", Journal of Black Studies, Vol. 9, No. 3, March, 1979, pp. 291-310.

340. *Curl, Charles H. "Black Studies: Form and Content", CLA Journal, Vol. 13, No. 1, September, 1969, pp. 1-9.

341. *DALIZU, Egambi F. "Black Studies: Reflections on a New Colonial Situation in the University", Black Academy Review, Vol. 3, Nos. 1 & 2, Spring-Summer, 1972, pp. 107-116.

342. Daniel, Eleanor M. "The Black Studies Library at Ohio State University", Micropublishers, Vol. 10, No. 4, December, 1971, pp. 1-2.

343. Daniel, Jack L. "Towards Meaningful Black Studies", Crisis, Vol. 79, No. 8, October, 1972, 259-260.

344. *Daniel, Philip T. K. "A Survey of Black Studies Programs in Midwestern Colleges and Universities", Western Journal of Black Studies, Vol. 2, No. 4, Winter, 1978, pp. 296-303.

345. *_____. "Black Studies: Discipline or Field of Study?" Western Journal of Black Studies, Vol. 4, No. 3, Fall, 1980, pp. 195-200.

346. Daniel, Walter G. "Black Studies in American Education", Journal of Negro Education, Vol. 39, No. 3, Summer, 1970, pp. 189-191.

347. _____. "Education for Negroes in 1970", Journal of Negro Education, Vol. 39, No. 1, Winter, 1970, pp. 1-3.

348. Darnton, John. "New Black Studies at Yale (University) Cover Slavery Era and Up", New York Times, May 15, 1969, pp. 1,49.

349. Davidson, Douglas. "A Note on Black Studies Tenure and Promotion", Review of Black Political Economy, Vol. 10, No. 3, Spring, 1980, pp. 300-304.

350. *_____. "Liberal Ideology and Black Education", Journal of Afro-American Issues, Vol. 3, No. 3, Winter/Spring, 1973, pp. 307-313.

351. *Davis, Vincent, Leonard Cain, and Ray Rist. "The Developmental Process in Black Studies Programs: A Comparative Analysis", Northwestern Journal of African and Black American Studies, Vol. 1, No. 2, Fall, 1973, pp. 1-14.

352. "Day in the Troubled Life of U. S. Schools", U.S. News & World Report, Vol. 66, No. 4, January 27, 1969, p. 8.

353. "Demands of Black Students at University of Wisconsin", Washington Post, February 14, 1969, p. A-1.

354. Denton, Herbert H. "Black Studies Approved by (DC) School Board",
     Washington Post, February 13, 1969, pp. F-1, F-2.

355. _____. "(Black Studies) Program Splits City College",
     Washington Post, March 6, 1969, pp. A-1, A-10.

356. Dillon, Merton L. "White Faces and Black Studies", Commonweal,
     Vol. 91, No. 17, January 30, 1970, pp. 476-479.

357. Dixon, Norman R. "Toward a Definition a Black Education", Negro
     Educational Review, Vol. 24, Nos. 3 & 4, July-October, 1973,
     pp. 114-115.

358. Dodson, Howard. "Needed: A New Perspective on Black History",
     Humanities (Published by NEH), Vol. 2, No. 1, February, 1981,
     pp. 1-2.

359. Doherty, Ann S. "Black Studies: A Report For Librarians", College
     and Research Libraries, Vol. 31, No. 6, November, 1970, pp. 384-386.

360. Donadlo, Stephen. "Black Power at Columbia (University)",
     Commentary, Vol. 46, No. 3, September, 1968, pp. 67-76.

361. Drimmer, Melvin. "Teaching Black History in America: What Are
     the Problems?" Negro History Bulletin, Vol. 33, No. 2, February,
     1970, 32-34.

362. Driver, Christopher. "The Colour of the Campus", Guardian Weekly,
     April, 1969, p. 7.

363.*DuBois, William E. B. "The Study of the Negro Problems", Annals of
     the American Academy of Political and Social Science, Vol. 11, No.
     1, January, 1898, pp. 1-23.

364. Dunbar, Ernest. "Black Revolt Hits the White Campus", Look, Vol.
     31, No. 22, October 31, 1967, pp. 27-31.

365. _____. "The Black Studies Thing", New York Times Magazine,
     April 6, 1969, pp. 25-26, 60, 65, 68, 75.

366. Dunlap, Lillian Rae. "Afro-American Studies Is Alive and Growing
     at Indiana", Black Collegian, Vol. 7, No. 3, January/February,
     1977, pp. 24, 62-63.

367. Durley, Gerald L. "Center for Black Students on University Campuses",
     Journal of Higher Education, Vol. 40, No. 6, June, 1969, pp. 473-
     476.

368. EARLY, Tracy, "Religion: Key Aspect of Black Studies Program",
     New York News World, January 31, 1981.

369. Easum, Donald B. "The Call for Black Studies", Africa Report,
     Vol. 14, Nos. 5 & 6, May-June 1969, pp. 16-23.

370.*Eckman, Fern Marja. "Black Studies: A Report", New York Post,
     April 20, 1970, p. 29, Article I, April 20, 1970, p. 29; Article
     II, April 21, 1970, p. 29; Article III, April 22, 1970, p. 45,
     Article IV, April 23, 1970, p. 48; Article V, April 24, 1970, p.
     46; Article VI, April 25, 1970, p. 46.

371. Editorial. "Black Mood on Campus", Life, Vol. 66, No. 4, January
     31, 1969, p. 32.

372. Editorial. "Black Studies Programs", Christianity Today, Vol. 13,
     No. 12, March 14, 1969, p. 25.

373. Editorial. "Black Studies Should Be, Not Stop", Carolinian,
     January 2, 1971, p. 4.

374. Editorial. "Black Studies: The Antioch Case", Antioch Review,
     Vol. 29, No. 2, Summer, 1969, pp. 143-144.

375. Editorial. "Say It Isn't So: Self Segregation by Black Students",
     New Republic, Vol. 160, No. 21, May 24, 1969, pp. 7-8.

376. Editorial. "Standards for Black Studies: Society for Religion in
     Higher Education Meeting at Wells College", Christian Century,
     Vol. 86, No. 37, September 10, 1969, p. 1153.

377.*Editorial. "Student Strikes: 1968-69", Black Scholar, Vol. 1,
     Nos. 3-4, January-February, 1970, pp. 65-75.

378. Editorial. "Teaching Black Studies With Independent Study", Negro
     History Bulletin, Vol. 34, No. 1, January, 1971, pp. 4-5.

379. Eisen, Jonathan. "Black Culture at Oberlin", Commonweal, Vol. 87,
     No. 22, March 8, 1968, pp. 676-677.

380.*Eko, Ewa U. "Consortium Approach to Developing African and Afro-
     American Studies, An Assessment", Journal of Afro-American Issues,
     Vol. 2, No. 1, Winter, 1974, pp. 35-47.

381. Elliott, Raymond N., Jr. and Leona Ferrer. "Black History",
     Elementary School Journal, Vol. 70, No. 5, February, 1970, pp. 279-
     283.

382. Engs, Robert F. "Black Studies", New Jersey Educational Review,
     Vol. 45, January, 1972, pp. 16-18.

383. _____. and John B. Williams. "Blacks on Campus: Integration
     By Evasion", Nation, Vol. 209, No. 17, November 17, 1969, pp. 537-
     540.

384. "Engulfed by Black Anger", Time, Vol. 93, No. 3, January 17, 1969,
     p. 46.

385. "Exclude Whites? No, Says Top Negro Educator", U.S. News & World
     Report, Vol. 66, No. 22, June 2, 1969, p. 18.

386. "FACULTY Backs Black Studies at U. of Wis." Washington Evening Star, March 4, 1969, p. A-1.

387. "Faculty Statement on Black Studies and on Establishing an All-Black University at Atlanta University", Atlanta University Bulletin, July, 1969, pp. 21-23.

388. Fenton, Edwin. "Crispus Attucks is Not Enough", Bulletin of the National Association of Secondary School Principals, Vol. 54, No. 2, 1970, pp. 7-14.

389. Fenton, Edwin. "Crispus Attucks Is Not Enough: The Social Studies and Black Americans", Social Education, Vol. 33, No. 4, April, 1969, pp. 396-399.

390. Filter, Paul A. "A Survey of Black Studies: Position and Opinions", Educational Leadership, Vol. 28, No. 4, January 1971, pp. 369-371.

391.*Fischer, Roger A. "Ghetto and Gown: The Birth of Black Studies", Current History, Vol. 57, No. 339, 1969, pp. 290-294, 299-300.

392. Fiske, Edward B. "Black Studies", Ann Arbor News, March 2, 1983, pp. F-1, F-2.

393. _____. "Black Studies Mark Gains But Seek Wider Role", New York Times, June 19, 1977, p. 38.

394. _____. "For Black Studies, The Fight Goes On", New York Times, January 13, 1983.

395.*Ford, Nick Aaron. "Attitudes and Actions of English Departments Toward the Promotion of Black Studies", CLA Journal, Vol. 16, No. 3, March, 1973, pp. 334-344.

396. _____. "Black Studies Programs", Current History, Vol. 67, No. 399, November, 1974, pp. 224-227, 233.

397. Fox, Sylvan. "City College Faculty Endorses Black Studies and Recruiting of the Poor", New York Times, June 15, 1969, pp. 1, 19.

398. _____. "City College Faculty Opposes 2 (Negro and Puerto Rican Studies) Demands", New York Times, June 11, 1969, pp. 1, 31.

399. Fraser, C. Gerald. "Scholars See Better Programs for Black Studies in College", New York Times, October 31, 1971.

400. Freedman, Mitchell. "Students (at Stony Brook) Rally Over Black Studies (Chairman Leslie Owens' Resignation)", Garden City (NY) Newsday, October 6, 1979.

401. Friedland, W. H. "Confrontation at Cornell", Trans-Action, Vol. 6, No. 6, June 1969, pp. 29-36.

402.*Frye, Charles A. "Black Studies as Individuation", JuJu, Vol. 1, No. 2, February, 1974.

403.*_____. "Black Studies: Definition and Administrative Model", Western Journal of Black Studies, Vol. 1, No. 2, June, 1977, pp. 93-97.

404. _____. "Higher Education in the New Age: The Role of Interdisciplinary Studies", American Theosophist, March, 1977, pp. 61-64.

405. "Full Black Program Urged at UR (University of Rochester)", Rochester Democrat and Chronicle, February 18, 1970, p. 5B.

406. Fuller, Hoyt W. "Black Images and White Critics", Negro Digest, Vol. 19, No. 10, November, 1969, p. 49.

407.*Furniss, W. T. "Black Studies and Civil Rights Violations", American Council of Education Special Report, April 18, 1969.

408.*_____. "Racial Minorities and Curriculum Change", Educational Record, Vol. 50, Fall, 1969, pp. 360-370.

409. GAYLE, Addison. "Blueprint For Black Criticism", First World, Vol. 1, No. 1, January/February, 1977, pp. 41-45.

410. Gentry, Afron and Robert L. Woodbury. "Why Black History", New England Social Studies Bulletin, Vol. 26, No. 1, Fall, 1969, pp. 10-13.

411. "Georgetown Adds Black Courses", Washington Post, August 16, 1969, p. D-8.

412. Genovese, Eugene D. "Black Studies: Trouble Ahead", Atlantic Monthly, Vol. 223, No. 6, June, 1969, pp. 37-41.

413. Gibson, E. F. "Three D's: Distortion, Deletion, Denial", Social Education, Vol. 33, No. 4, April, 1969, pp. 406-409.

414. Gilpin, Patrick J. and O. Kendall White, Jr. "A Challenge to White Southern Universities-An Argument for Including Negro History in the Curriculum", Journal of Negro Education, Vol. 39, No. 4, Summer, 1969, pp. 443-446.

415. Ginzberg, Eli. "Black Power and Student Unrest: Reflections on Columbia University and Harlem", George Washington Law Review, Vol. 37, May, 1969, pp. 835-847.

416.*Goldman, Martin S. "Black Arrival in American History: A Historiographical Look at the Sixties", Social Studies, Vol. 62, No. 5, October, 1971, pp. 209-219.

417.*_____. "The Academic Subversion of Black Studies", Social Studies, Vol. 65, No. 1, January, 1974, pp. 26-34.

418.*Goldstein, Rhoda Lois and June True Albert. "The Status of Black Studies Programs on American Campuses, 1969-1971", Journal of Social and Behavioral Sciences, Vol. 20, No. 1, Winter, 1974, pp. 1-16.

419. Goodman, George J. "White Dentist (Dr. Daniel Jay Perlman) in Harlem (NY) Will Teach Black Studies", New York Times, September 11, 1972.

420. Gordon, Edmund W. "A Black Educator's Case For Ethnic Studies", College Board Review, No. 85, February, 1972, pp. 24-28.

421. Grange, Hamlin. "The Viability of Black Studies at the University of Colorado", Black Collegian, Vol. 7, No. 3, January/February, 1977, pp. 22-23.

422. Gross, Kenneth G. "Blacks on Campus: Angry and Alone Together", Nation, Vol. 208, No. 7, February 17, 1969, pp. 207-210.

423.*Grossman, Jonathan. "Black Studies in the Department of Labor, 1897-1907", Monthly Labor Review, Vol. 97, No. 6, June, 1974, pp. 17-27.

424.*Guinier, Ewart. "Black Studies: Training for Leadership", Freedomways, Vol. 15, No. 3, Third Quarter, 1975, pp. 196-205.

425. _____. "Black Studies: Understanding the U.S.A.", Crisis, Vol. 88, No. 2, May, 1981, pp. 83-87.

426. HALE, Irlene W. "Black Culture", Clearing House, Vol. 45, No. 5, January, 1971, pp. 269-271.

427. Hale, Janice E. "De-mythicizing the Education of Black Children", First World, Vol. 1, No. 3, May/June, 1977, pp. 30-35.

428. Hamilton, Charles V. "The Challenge of Black Studies", Social Policy, Vol. 1, No. 2, 1970, pp. 14-16.

429. _____. "The Question of Black Studies", Phi Delta Kappan, Vol. 51, March, 1970, pp. 362-368.

430. Handler, M.S. "Hunter (College) Is Offering Black Studies Degree Courses", New York Times, October 26, 1969.

431. Hannah, Marguerite G. "Black Studies", Hilltop (Howard University), October 7, 1977, p. 10.

432. Harding, Vincent. "Achieving Educational Equality: Stemming the Black Brain Drain", Current, Vol. 105, No. 10, March, 1969, pp. 37-40.

433. _____. "Black Brain Drain", Columbia Forum, Winter, 1968, pp. 38-39.

434. _____. "Black Students and the Impossible Revolution", Ebony, Vol. 24, No. 10, August, 1969, pp. 141-149.

435. _____. "New Creation or Familiar Death: An Open Letter to Black Students in the North", Negro Digest, Vol. 28, No. 3, March, 1969, pp. 5-14.

436.*Hare, Nathan. "Questions and Answers About Black Studies", Massachusetts Review, Vol. 10, No. 4, Autumn, 1969, pp. 727-736.

437.* _____. "The Struggle of Black Students", Journal of Afro-American Issues, Vol. 1, No. 2, Fall, 1972, pp. 111-113.

438. _____. "The Teaching of Black History and Culture in the Secondary Schools", Social Education, Vol. 33, No. 4, April, 1969, pp. 385-389.

439.* _____. "What Black Studies Mean to the Black Scholar", College University Business, Vol. 48, May 1970, pp. 56-61.

440.* _____. "What Should Be the Role of Afro-American Education in the Undergraduate Curriculum?" Liberal Education, Vol. 55, No. 1, March, 1969, pp. 42-50.

441. Harlan, Louis R. "Tell It Like It Was, Suggestions on Black History", Social Education, Vol. 33, No. 4, April, 1969, pp. 390-395.

442. Haro, Roberto P. "Toward a Typology of Ethnic Studies Programs", Journal of Society of Ethnic and Special Studies, Vol. 5, No. 1, Fall, 1980, pp. 3-10.

443. Harper, Frederick D. "Developing a Curriculum of Self-Esteem For Black Youth", Journal of Negro Education, Vol. 46, No. 2, Spring, 1977, pp. 133-140.

444.* _____. "Media For Change: Black Students in the White University", Journal of Negro Education, Vol. 40, No. 3, Summer, 1971, pp. 255-265.

445. Harris, Jeanette H., "The Black Studies Crisis", Negro History Bulletin, Vol. 34, No. 1, January, 1971, pp. 6-9.

446. Harris, Nelson H. "The Treatment of Negroes in Books and Media Designed for the Elementary Schools", Social Education, Vol. 33, No. 4, April, 1969, pp. 435-437.

447.*Harris, Robert L., Jr. "Segregation and Scholarship: The American Council of Learned Societies' Committee on Negro Studies, 1941-1950", Journal of Black Studies, Vol. 12, No. 3, March, 1982, pp. 315-331.

448. Harris, Sheldon. "San Fernando Black Revolt", Commonweal, Vol. 89, No. 17, January 31, 1969, pp. 549-552.

449.*Harrison, Charles H. "Black History and the Schools", Ebony, Vol. 24, No. 2, December, 1968, pp. 111-122.

450.*Harrison, E. C. "Student Unrest on the Black Campus", Journal of Negro Education, Vol. 41, No. 2, Spring, 1972, pp. 113-120.

451. "Harvard Opens Black Study", New York Times, September 22, 1969, 1, 84.

452. Hatch, John. "Black Studies: The Real Issue", Nation, Vol. 20, No. 24, June 16, 1969, pp. 755-758.

453. Hawkins, Homer C. and Thomas S. Gunnings. "Bi-Cultural Education: A Necessity", Journal of Afro-American Issues, Vol. 1, No. 3, Winter/Spring, 1973, pp. 267-272.

454. Hayakawa, S. I. "The Meaning of Black Studies", On The Record (SFC Pamphlet 70-S), April 1, 1970, p. 1.

455.*Hechinger, Fred M. "Black Studies Come of Age", New York Times, April 13, 1980, pp. 60-62, 68, 73.

456. Henshel, Anne M. and Richard L. Henshel. "Black Studies Program: Promise and Pitfalls", Journal of Negro Education, Vol. 38, No. 4, Fall, 1969, pp. 423-429.

457. Herbert, Bob. "Black Studies Running Rough Course", New York Daily News, February 24, 1980, p. 2-H.

458.*Herskovits, Melville J. "Problems, Method and Theory in Afro-merican Studies", Afroamerica, Vol. 1, Nos. 1-2, January-June, 1945.

459.*_____. "The Contribution of Afroamerican Studies to Africanist Research", American Anthropologist, Vol. 50, No. 1, January-March, 1948, pp. 1-10.

460.*_____. "The Interdisciplinary Aspects of Negro Studies", American Council of Learned Societies Bulletin, Vol. 32, 1941, pp. 339-347.

461.*_____. "The Present Status and Needs For Afro-American Research", Journal of Negro History, Vol. 36, No. 2, April, 1951, pp. 123-147.

462. Holtzman, Wayne N. "Private Foundations and Black Professionals (Establishing Black Studies Programs)", Journal of Afro-American Issues, Vol. 1, No. 3, Winter/Spring, 1973, pp. 276-277.

463.*Hoover, Dwight W. "The Black Past as Reflection of the American Present", Michigan Academicians, Vol. 2, No. 3, 1970, pp. 49-62.

464. "How to Integrate Your District's Curriculum", School Management, Vol. 12, No. 8, August, 1968, pp. 20-25.

465. Hunter, Charlayne. "Confusion Feared in Black Studies", New York Times, March 8, 1970, pp. 58.

466. Hurt, N. Franklin. "Put the Negro into United States History", Illinois Education, Vol. 56, March, 1968, pp. 288-290.

467. "IDEAS for Teaching About Black Americans", Negro History Bulletin, Vol. 3, No. 2, February, 1971, pp. 35-36.

468.*Ijere, Martin O. "Whither Economics in a Black Studies Program?" Journal of Black Studies, Vol. 3, No. 2, December, 1972, pp. 149-165.

469. "Illinois Council For Black Studies Call For Moratorium on Black Studies", Chicago Defender, April 13, 1981, p. 9.

470. "It Can't Happen Here, Can It?" Newsweek, Vol. 73, No. 18, May 5, 1969, pp. 26-30.

471. Ivie, Standley D. "Are Black Studies Relevant?" Education Forum, Vol. 37, No. 2, January, 1973.

472. "Ivy League Boost for Black Studies", U.S. News & World Report, Vol. 66, No. 5, February 3, 1969, p. 10.

473. JACKSON, Maurice. "Toward a Sociology of Black Studies", Journal of Black Studies, Vol. 1, No. 2, December, 1970, pp. 131-140.

474. Jarolimek, John. "Social Studies, The Elementary School Focus on Minority Groups", Social Education, Vol. 33, No. 4, April, 1969, pp. 429-433.

475. Jeffries, Leonard. "The Essence of Black Studies", City College Alumnus, April, 1982, pp. 10-13.

476. Johnson, Berman E. "Black Awareness vs. Black History on the College Campus", Negro History Bulletin, Vol. 45, No. 3, July-August-September, 1982, pp. 60-61.

477. Johnson, Ronald M. "Black History and White Students: Broadening Cultural Horizons", Negro Educational Review, Vol. 28, No. 1, January, 1977, pp. 13-18.

478.*Johnson, Roosevelt. "Blacks and Higher Education - A Decade in Review", Journal of Afro-American Issues, Vol. 5, No. 1, Winter, 1977, pp. 88-97.

479. Johnson, Thomas A. "Campus Racial Tensions Rise as Black Enrollment Increases", New York Times, April 4, 1972.

480. _____. "Educators Find Black Studies Are Changing Higher Education", New York Times, June 4, 1972.

481. Johnson, Whittington B. and Ted Nicholas. "Black Studies: A Key to the Future", Journal of Negro Education, Vol. 46, No. 2, Spring, 1977, pp. 118-123.

482. Johnston, Percy E. "Black Researchers and Afro-American Mathematicians", Afro-American Journal of Philosophy, Vol. 1, No. 4, Spring, 1983, pp. 129-132.

483.* _____. Editorial. "Black Press: Philosophy Journals and Philosophical Journals", Afro-American Journal of Philosophy, Vol. 1, No. 1, Summer, 1982, pp. 21-28.

484. _____. "Problems of Afro-American Scholars: William Thomas Fontaine's Notions", Afro-American Journal of Philosophy, Vol. 1, No. 1, Summer, 1982, pp. 21-28.

485.*Jones, Rhett S. "From Pawn to Person: History, The Social Sciences and the Evolving Image of Afro-Americans", Free Inquiry, Vol. 4, November, 1976, pp. 152-170.

486. _____. "History, Social Structure and Psyche: Toward a Black Psychology", Journal of the Pan-African Studies Society, Vol. 1, Spring/Summer, 1978, pp. 18-25.

487.*_____. "Training Graduate Students in Black History: Some Methodological Strategies", Négro Educational Review, Vol. 26, No. 1, January, 1975, pp. 5-21.

488. _____. "Understanding Afro-American Thought: Can the Black Writer Help?" Studies in Black Literature, Vol. 7, Spring, 1976, pp. 10-15.

489.*Jovanick, William. "The American Textbook: An Unscientific Phenomenon-Quality Without Control", American Scholar, Vol. 38, No. 2, 1969, pp. 227-239.

490. Just, Ward. "What Is This 'Black Studies', What's All the Fuss About?" Washington Post, March 17, 1969, p. A-1.

491.*KAISER, Ernest. "The History of Negro History", Negro Digest, Vol. 17, No. 2, February, 1968.

492.*Kamoche, Jidlaph G. "The Interdepartmental and Autonomous Types of Afro-American Studies Program: A Comparative Perspective on Personnel Strengths and Weaknesses", UMOJA, Vol. 4, No. 4, Spring, 1980, pp. 21-39.

493.*Karenga, Maulana Ron. "Corrective History: Reconstructing The Black Past", First World, Vol. 1, No. 3, May/June, 1977, pp. 50-54.

494.*Katz, William A. "The State of Black Studies in U. S. Schools Today: An Interview With Professor LaMar P. Miller", Equal Opportunity Review, April, 1973.

495. Katz, William Loren. "Black History in Secondary Schools", Journal of Negro Education, Vol. 38, No. 4, Summer, 1969, pp. 430-434.

496. Kaurouma, Patricia. "Resources For Researching Afro-American Geneaology", Afro-Americans in New York Life and History, Vol. 1, No. 2, July, 1977, pp. 217-224.

497. Keith, Leroy. "Issues Facing Black Students and Faculty at Predominantly White Institutions", Journal of Afro-American Issues, Vol. 1, No. 1, Summer, 1972, pp. 69-73.

498. Kerby, Elizabeth. "Struggle For a Black Perspective", The UCLA Review, Vol. 10, No. 4, 1970, pp. 1-4.

499.*Kilson, Martin. "Anatomy of the Black Studies Movement", Massachusetts Review, Vol. 10, No. 4, Autumn, 1969, pp. 718-725.

500. _____. "Black Studies and Black Militants", West Africa, October 1, 1971, pp. 1139-1140.

501. _____. "Black Studies Movement: A Plea for Perspective", Crisis, Vol. 76, No. 8, October, 1969, pp. 327-332.

502.*_____ . "Reflections on Structure and Content in Black Studies", Journal of Black Studies, Vol. 3, No. 3, March, 1973, pp. 297-314.

503. _____. "The Black Experience at Harvard", New York Times Magazine, September 2, 1973, pp. 13f+.

504. King, George D. "Black Studies: An Idea in Crisis", Western Journal of Black Studies, Vol. 6, No. 4, Winter, 1982, pp. 241-245.

505.*King, William M. "Black Studies Challenge the Myths", Colorado Quarterly, Vol. 22, No. 2, Winter, 1973, pp. 169-178.

506. Kraft, Joseph. "(Vietnam) War Yields to Black Studies As a Campus Trouble Starter", Washington Post, February 13, 1969.

507. Krim, Robert M. "Harvard Expected to Approve Program of Black Studies", Washington Post, February 10, 1969, p. A-1.

508. "Kurt Schmoke on Black Studies", Baltimore Sun, December 17, 1970, Section K, p. 2.

509. LAFRANCHI, Howard. "Black Studies Today: Though Caught in Some Squeezes, Afro-American History is Here to Stay", Christian Science Monitor, February, 1984, pp. 23, 25.

510. Larder, James. "Rift in the Ranks: Scholars Split Sharply Over the Role of Black Studies", Washington Post, December 3, 1982, pp. E-1, E-9.

511. Lawson, James R. "Black University Concept: Educators' Response", Negro Digest, Vol. 18, No. 3, March, 1969, pp. 66-68.

512. _____. "Student Participation in Educational Change", Journal of Negro Education, Vol. 40, No. 3, Summer, 1971, pp. 282-289.

513. Lee, Carleton L. "Black Americana Studies", Negro History Bulletin, Vol. 34, No. 5, May, 1971, pp. 114-115.

514. Lerner, Abba P. "Black Studies: The Universities in Moral Crisis", Humanist, Vol. 29, No. 3, May-June, 1969, pp. 9-104.

515.*Lewis, W. Arthur. "The Road to the Top is Through Higher Education -- Not Black Studies", New York Times Magazine, May 11, 1969, pp. 34, 53.

516. Lindberg, John. "Discovering Black Literature", North American Review, Vol. 6, No. 3, 1969, pp. 51-56.

517. Litcher, John H. and David W. Johnson. "Changes in Attitudes of
     White Elementary School Students After Use of Multi-Ethnic Readers",
     Journal of Educational Psychology, Vol. 60, No. 2, April, 1969,
     pp. 148-152.

518. Litwak, Leo, "Battle For a College: Why San Francisco State Blew
     Up: We Need A Revolution", Look, Vol. 33, No. 11, May 27, 1969,
     pp. 61-62, 65-66.

519. Locke, O.C. "Art and Black Studies", School Arts, September, 1972,
     pp. 46-47.

520. Long, Richard. "The Black Studies Boondoggle", Liberator, Vol. 10,
     No. 9, September, 1970, pp. 6-9.

521.*Love, Theresa R. "From Black Studies to Ethnic Studies Programs in
     American Colleges and Universities", Journal of Afro-American Is-
     sues, Vol. 5, No. 1, Winter, 1977, pp. 51-59.

522. Lythcott, Stephen. "The Case for Black Studies", Antioch Review,
     Vol. 29, No. 2, Summer, 1969, pp. 149-154.

523. MACK, John B. III. "Black Studies and the Library", Illinois Li-
     braries, Vol. 52, No. 7, Spring, 1970, pp. 641-646.

524. Mackey, James. "A Rationale for Black Studies", Social Studies,
     Vol. 61, No. 7, 1970, pp. 323-325.

525. Malcolm X. "Afro-American History", International Socialist Review,
     Vol. 28, No. 2, March-April, 1964, pp. 4-8.

526. Malveaux, J. "Black Studies: An Assessment", Essence, Vol. 11, No.
     8, August, 1980, pp. 78-79.

527. Matthews, John."Directorship Disputed: City College Black Studies
     Issue Boils", Washington Sunday Star, March 9, 1969, p. A-1.

528. Matthews, John."5 on Black Study Staff (Federal City College) Pre-
     sumed to Have Quit", Washington Evening Star, July 25, 1969, p.
     A-1.

529. _____ . and Ernest Holsendolph. "When Black Studies Take Over
     a Campus", New Republic, Vol. 158, No. 15, April 13, 1968, p. 10.

530. Mauk, Marion. "Black Studies: San Francisco State Courses", New
     Republic, Vol 160, No. 11, March 15, 1969, pp. 12-13.

531. Mayes, J. P. "Comments From Black Studies Majors: Graduates and
     Undergraduates; Black Studies, Meaningful or Bogus?" Mzalendo
     (Ohio State University), Vol. 1, No. 1, Autumn/Winter, 1977-1978,
     pp. 1, 3-4.

532.*McBride, Ullysses. "The Status of Black Studies in Traditionally
     Black Institutions in America", Negro Educational Review, Vol. 25,
     No. 4, October, 1974, pp. 208-212.

533. McClendon, William H. "Ethnic Education For Liberation: The Mission of Black Studies", Northwest Journal of African and Black American Studies, Vol. 1, No. 1, Summer, 1973, pp. 3-6.

534. McEachen, Gaye. "Afro-American History: Schools Rush to Get in Step", Nation's Schools, Vol. 82, No. 9, September, 1968, pp. 58-63, 94.

535. McLaughlin, Maurice. "Alexandria (VA) Black Study Sit-in Ends", Washington Post, April 17, 1969, p. A-1.

536. Melman, Seymour. "Economic Development or Race War", Columbia Daily Spectator, April 30, 1969.

537. Meyers, Michael. "Black Separation at Antioch: A Retrospective View", Civil Liberties, No. 227, April, 1971, pp. 4-6.

538. Milkereit, John E. "Building Takeovers at the University of Akron: Shots Fired in Buchtel Hall", School and Society, Vol. 98, No. 2327, October, 1970, pp. 374-375.

539. *Miller, Larmar P. "Black Studies, A New Area of Instruction", American Association of School Administrators, February 18, 1970.

540. Millner, Darrell. "Black Studies Instruction: New Perceptions", Western Journal of Black Studies, Vol. 1, No. 1, March, 1977, pp. 46-51.

541. Mintz, Sidney W. "Creating Culture in the Americas", Columbia Forum, Spring, 1970, pp. 4-11.

542. *_____. "Towards an Afro-American History", Journal of History, Vol. 8, 1971, pp. 317-332.

543. Moorman, Elliott D. "The Benefit of Anger", Saturday Review, Vol. 52, No. 25, June 21, 1969, pp. 72-73, 84.

544. "Mount Vernon, NY to Demand Negro History Be Made Part of Regular History Curriculum", New York Times, February 17, 1969, p. 30.

545. Mullen, James H. "Racial Tensions on Campus", Pan-African Journal, Vol. 3, No. 1, 1970, pp. 30-33.

546. NAEEM, Abdul Basit. "Says Black Studies Programs Should Include Studies on (Elijah) Muhammed's Mission", Muhammed Speaks, May 16, 1969, p. 4.

547. "(Nathan) Hare Drops Demand To Head Black Studies", Washington Post, August 28, 1969.

548. "Negro at Yale: New Course on Negro in America", Newsweek, Vol. 72, No. 26, December 23, 1968, p. 62.

549. "Negroes Demand Black Studies (At San Francisco College)", New York Times, December 7, 1968, p. 31.

550. Nelson, Bryce. "Brandeis: How a Liberal University Reacts to a Black Take-Over", Science, Vol. 163, No. 3874, March 28, 1969, pp. 1431-1434.

551.*Newton, James E. "A Review of Black Studies As Related To Basic Elements of Curriculum", Afro-American Studies, Vol. 3, No. 4, 1975, pp. 255-260.

552.*_____. "A Review of Black Studies As Related to Basic Elements of Curriculum", Journal of Negro Education, Vol. 43, No. 4, Fall, 1974, pp. 477-488.

553. Neyland, Leedell W. "Why Negro History in the Junior and Senior High School?" Social Studies, Vol. 58, No. 7, 1967, pp. 315-321.

554. "North Carolina Central (N.C.C.U.) To Offer Black Studies", Raleigh News and Observer, March 28, 1970.

555. Nuru, Njeri H. "The Challenge of Black English", Chronicle of Higher Education, Vol. 21, No. 13, November 17, 1980, p. 24.

556. "NYC RC Archdiocese Parochial Schools to Give Course on Negro History in America Beginning in September", New York Times, July 3, 1969, p. 18.

557. OBATALA, J. K. "Black Studies Stop the Shouting and Go To Work", Smithsonian, Vol. 5, No. 9, December, 1974, pp. 46-53.

558. O'Brien, David J. "Black History and Color Blind Men", Catholic World, Vol. 208, No. 1243, 1968, pp. 29-32.

559. Okoye, F. Nwabueze. "The Relationship Between African and Afro-American Studies", Negro History Bulletin, Vol. 41, No. 5, September-October, 1978, pp. 881-882.

560. "Ohio State U. To Offer Negro History Course", New York Times, May 10, 1969, P. 38.

561. Overbea, Luix. "Black Studies: Will They Make the Grade?" Christian Science Monitor, September 21, 1979, p. 6.

562. _____. "Making Black History Part of the Historical Mainstream?" Christian Science Monitor, February 14, 1983, p. 16.

563. _____. "Start Your Own Black History Studies", Christian Science Monitor, February 14, 1983, 16.

564. Owens, Bill. "A New Beginning Toward A More Productive Future For Black Studies", Contributions in Black Studies: Journal of African and Afro-American Studies, No. 3, 1979-1980, pp. 39-43.

565. PACHTER, Henry. "Teaching Negro History", Dissent, Vol. 16, No. 2, March-April, 1969, pp. 151-156.

566.*Patterson, Orlando, "Rethinking Black History", Harvard Educational Review, Vol. 41, No. 3, August, 1971, pp. 297-315.

567. "Penna. U. to Offer Credit Course in History of Negro in America", New York Times, March 20, 1969, p. 40.

568. Penteny, Devere. "Case for Black Studies", Atlantic Monthly, Vol. No. 4, April, 1969, pp. 81-82.

569. Peterson, Iver. "Black Studies Open to All Races, Is Approved at Penn", New York Times, April 7, 1972.

570. Pickens, William G. "Teaching Negro Culture in High Schools - Is It Worthwhile?" Journal of Negro Education, Vol. 34, No. 2, Spring, 1965, pp. 106-113.

571.*Picott, Rupert J. "Black Studies: Comment", Negro History Bulletin, Vol. 36, No. 2, February, 1973, p. 28.

572. Pogue, Frank G. "Graduate Education in African and Afro-American Studies: An Assessment at SUNY in Albany", Western Journal of Black Studies, Vol. 1, No. 2, June, 1977, pp. 87-92.

573. Poinsett, Alex. "Plight of Black Studies", Ebony, Vol. 29, No. 2, December, 1973, pp. 128-130.

574. _____. "Think Tank for Black Scholars", Ebony, Vol. 25, No. 4, February, 1970, pp. 46-48.

575.*Porter, Curtiss E. "An Education(al) Insight: Black World; What Have We Not Done to Define Black Studies in the Terms by Which We Exist", Black Lines: A Journal of Black Studies, Vol. 1, No. 4, Summer, 1971, pp. 53-64.

576. Porter, Dorothy. "Bibliography and Research in Afro-American Scholarship", Journal of Academic Librarianship, Vol. 11, May, 1978, pp. 77-81.

577. Poussaint, Alvin and Carolyn Atkinson. "Black Youth and Motivation", Black Scholar, Vol. 1, No. 5, March, 1970, pp. 43-51.

578. "Problems of Negro-College Students", Trans-Action, Vol. 5, No. 4, March, 1968, p. 9.

579. "Protest and Authority: Symposium", Newsweek, Vol. 33, No. 19, May 12, 1969, pp. 72-73.

580. Psencik, Leroy F. "Teaching About the Negro in Social Studies - A Guide to Sources", Social Studies, Vol. 61, No. 5, 1970, pp. 195-200.

581. "Putting 'Soul' Into History", America, May 10, 1969, p. 5.

582. "Puzzled About Afro-American Culture?" U.S. News & World Report, Vol. 66, No. 8, February 24, 1969, pp. 52-54.

583.*QUARLES, Benjamin. "Black History Unbound", Daedalus, Vol. 103, No. 2, 1974, pp. 163-178.

584.*RAFKY, David M. "Attitudes of Black Studies Faculty Toward Black Students: A National Survey", Journal of College Student Personnel, Vol. 14, No. 1, January, 1973, pp. 25-30.

585.*_____. "Student Militance: A Dilemma For Black Faculty", Journal of Black Studies, Vol. 3, No. 2, December, 1972, pp. 183-206.

586. Raspberry, William. "Do Blacks Now Seek Separatism?" Washington Post, August 29, 1970, p. A-15.

587.*Ray, LeRoi R., Jr. "Black Studies: Discussion of Evaluation", Journal of Negro Education, Vol. 45, No. 4, Fall, 1976, pp. 383-397.

588. Record, Wilson. "Black Studies and White Sociologists", American Sociologists, Vol. 7, No. 5, May, 1972, pp. 10-11.

589.*_____. "Can Black Studies and Sociology Find Common Ground?" Journal of Negro Education, Vol. 44, No. 1, Winter, 1973, pp. 63-83.

590.*_____. "Response of Sociologists to Black Studies", Journal of Higher Education, Vol. 45, No. 5, May, 1974, pp. 364-391.

591.*_____. "Some Implications of the Black Studies Movement For Higher Education in the 1960's", Journal of Higher Education, Vol. 44, No. 3, March, 1973, pp. 191-216.

592.*_____. "White Sociologists and Black Students in Predominantly White Universities", Sociological Quarterly, Vol. 15, No. 2, Spring, 1974, pp. 164-182.

593. Redding, J. Saunders. "Afro-American Studies", New York Times Book Review, September 20, 1970, p. 19.

594.*_____. "The Black Revolution in American Studies", American Studies International, Vol. 17, No. 4, Summer, 1979, pp. 8-14.

595. _____. "The Black Youth Movement", American Scholar, Vol. 28, No. 4, Autumn, 1969, pp. 584-587.

596. "Reed College Bars Autonomous Center For Negro Studies", New York Times, January 27, 1969.

597.*Reid, Inez Smith. "Analysis of Black Studies Programs", Pan-African Journal, Vol. 2, No. 3, 1969, pp. 284-298.

598.*_____. "An Analysis of Black Studies Programs", Afro-American Studies, Vol. 1, No. 1, January, 1970, pp. 11-21.

599. Reinhold, Robert. "Harvard Report Calls For Degree in Negro Studies", New York Times, January 22, 1969, pp. 1, 22.

600. _____. "Professors Weigh Black Study Role", New York Times, June 25, 1972.

601. Rigsby, Gregory V. "Afro-American Studies at Howard University", Journal of Negro Education, Vol. 39, No. 3, Summer, 1970, pp. 209-212.

602.*Rist, Ray. "Black Staff, Black Studies at White Universities: Study in Contradiction", Journal of Higher Education, Vol. 41, No. 8, November, 1970, pp. 618-629.

603.* _____. "Black Studies and Paraprofessionals-A Prescription For Ailing Reading Programs in Urban Schools", Journal of Reading, Vol. 14, No. 8, May 1971, pp. 525-530, 583.

604. Rivers, Larry E. "PSI: An Alternative Approach to the Teaching of Black Studies", Western Journal of Black Studies, Vol. 3, No. 1, Spring, 1979, pp. 66-71.

605. Roberts, Stevens V. "Black Studies Aim to Change Things", New York Times, May 15, 1969, pp. 1, 93.

606. _____. "Black Studies: More Than Soul Courses", Commonweal, Vol. 91, No. 17, January 30, 1970, pp. 478-479.

607. Robinson, Carrie. "Media For the Black Curriculum", ALA Bulletin, Vol. 63, No. 1, February, 1969, pp. 242-246.

608. Robinson, Donald W. "European Textbooks and America's Racial Problem", Social Education, Vol. 33, No. 3, March, 1969, pp. 310-319.

609. Robinson, Walter G. and Gossie Harold Hudson. "Intellectual History Need: Black Thought In the Literature", Journal of Afro-American Issues, Vol. 1, No. 2, Fall, 1972, pp. 257-262.

610. Rosenthal, Michael, et.al. "Blacks at Brandeis", Commonweal, Vol. 89, No. 23, March 14, 1969, pp. 727-730.

611.*Rosovsky, Henry. "Black Studies at Harvard: Personal Reflections Concerning Recent Events", American Scholar, Vol. 38, No. 4, 1969, pp. 562-572.

612.*Rosser, James M. "Higher Education and the Black American: An Overview", Journal of Afro-American Issues, Vol. 1, No. 2, Fall, 1972, pp. 189-204.

613.* _____, and E. Thomas Copeland. "Reflections: Black Studies-Black Education?" Journal of Black Studies, Vol. 3, No. 3, March, 1973, pp. 287-295.

613a. Rossman, Michael. "Blacks at Mainstream U: The Problems of Desegregation", Commonweal, Vol. 89, No. 1, October 4, 1968, pp. 15-17.

614. Roth, Rodney W. "Critique of Developments (of Black Studies Movement) at the Elementary Level", Journal of Negro Education, Vol. 39, No. 3, Summer, 1970, pp. 230-238.

615. _____. "The Effects of 'Black Studies' On Negro Fifth Grade Students", Journal of Negro Education, Vol. 38, No. 3, Summer, 1969.

616.*Rousseve, Ronald J. "Dealing Responsibly With the Black American",
    Negro Educational Review, Vol. 20, No. 4, Cctober, 1969, pp. 95-
    105.

617.*Russell, Joseph, Jr. "Afro-American Studies: From Chaos to Consoli-
    dation", Negro Educational Review, Vol. 26, No. 4, October, 1974,
    pp. 181-189.

618.*Ryan, Pat M. "White Experts, Black Experts, and Black Studies",
    Black Academy Review, Vol. 2, No. 1, Spring, 1970, pp. 52-65.

619."SAN FRANCISCO State College to Cffer Program Leading to Degree in
    Negro Studies", New York Times, January 28, 1969, p. 16.

620.*"Scholars Split Cver the Role of Black Studies", Washington Post,
    December 3, 1982, p. E-1.

621. Schrag, Peter. "The New Black Myths", Harper's Magazine, Vol. 238,
    No. 1428, May, 1969, pp. 37-42.

622. Scully, Malcolm G. "Black Studies Plan Sparks Bitter Debate at Fe-
    deral City College", Chronicle of Higher Education, Vol. 3, No. 14,
    March 24, 1969, p. 5.

623.*Semmes, Clovis E. "Black Studies and the Symbolic Structure of Do-
    mination", Western Journal of Black Studies, Vol. 6, No. 2, Summer,
    1982, pp. 116-122.

624.*_____. "Foundations of an Afrocentric Social Science: Implica-
    tions for Curriculum-Building, Theory and Research in Black Studies",
    Journal of Black Studies, Vol. 12, No. 1, September, 1981, pp. 3-17.

625. "Shutdown at San Francisco State Black Students Union Members Riot",
    Time, Vol. 92, No. 21, November 22, 1968, p. 5.

626. Sievert, W. A. "Ethnic Studies: Vanishing, or Not? Report of the
    State Coordinating Council of Higher Education in California",
    Saturday Review of Education, Vol. 1, No. 1, February, 1973, p. 54.

627. Simon, Sidney and Alice Carnes. "Teaching Afro-American History
    With a Focus on Values", Educational Leadership, Vol. 27, No. 3,
    December, 1969, pp. 222-228.

628. Sims, William. "Black Studies: An Ecological Process", Western
    Journal of Black Studies, Vol. 1, No. 1, March, 1977, pp. 33-37.

629.*Sitton, Thad. "Black History From the Community: The Strategies of
    Fieldwork", Journal of Negro Education, Vol. 50, No. 2, Spring,
    1981, pp. 171-181.

630. Smith, Arthur L. "What's the Score on Black Studies?" Today's Edu-
    cation, Vol. 61, No. 1, January, 1972, p. 62.

631.*Smith, Jessie Carney. "The Impact of Black Studies Programs on the
    Academic Library", College and Research Library, Vol. 33, No. 2,
    March, 1972, pp. 87-96.

632.*Smith, William D. "Black Studies: A Survey of Models and Curricula", Journal of Black Studies, Vol. 1, No. 4, June, 1971, pp. 259-272.

633.* _____. "Black Studies: Recommendations For Organizations and National Consideration", Journal of Afro-American Issues, Vol. 1, No. 4, Summer/Fall, 1973, pp. 350-357.

634.* _____, and Albert C. Yates. Editorial. "Black Studies", Journal of Black Studies, Vol. 10, No. 3, March, 1980, pp. 269-277.

635.* _____. "The Opinions of Administrative Heads of Black Studies: A Summary", Phi Delta Kappan, Vol. 53, No. 7, March, 1972.

636.*Smith, William L. "Critique of Development (of Black Studies Movement) at the Secondary Level", Journal of Negro Education, Vol. 39, No. 3, Summer, 1970, pp. 239-261.

637. "Soul Brothers and Swahili", Newsweek, Vol. 70, No. 25, October 9, 1967, p. 59.

638. Sowell, Thomas and Ronald B. Bailey,"Opinions Differ on Black Studies: One Viewpoint", Today's Education, Vol. 63, No. 7, November,

639. Spaights, Ernest. "Black Studies Programs", Urban Review, Vol. 5, No. 1, 1971, pp. 38-41.

640.*Spratten, Thaddeus H. "The Educational Relevance of Black Studies-An Interdisciplinary and Inter-Cultural Interpretation", Western Journal of Black Studies, Vol. 1, No. 1, March, 1977, pp. 38-44.

641. Spurlock, Karla J. "The Value of a Major in African/Afro-American Studies", Habari Newsletter, (SUNY at Albany), Vol. 3, No. 2, January 27, 1977.

642. _____. "Toward the Evolution of a Unitary Disciplinary Concept of African/Afro-American Studies", Western Journal of Black Studies, Vol. 1, No. 3, September, 1977, pp. 224-228.

643. Steinberg, David. "Black Power and the Campus", National Review, Vol. 20, No. 40, October 8, 1968, pp. 1001-1004.

644. _____. "Black Power Roots on Black Campuses", Commonweal, Vol. 88, No. 5, April 19, 1968, pp. 127-128.

645. Stewart, James B. "Alternative Models For Black Studies", UMOJA, Vol. 5, 1981, pp. 19-20.

646. _____. "Black Studies and Black People in the Future", Black Book Bulletin, Summer, 1976, pp. 20-25.

647. _____. "Black Studies: Review Essay", Western Journal of Black Studies, Vol. 7, No. 2, Summer, 1983, pp. 113-117.

648. _____. "Educator Outlines Task of Black Studies", National Leader, October 13, 1983, pp. 12, 21.

649.* _____ . "Introducing Black Studies: A Critical Examination of Some Textual Materials", UMOJA, Vol. 3, No. 1, Spring, 1979, pp. 5-17.

650. Stone, Sonja H. "Black Studies Precept and Example: The Southeastern Black Press Institute", Western Journal of Black Studies, Vol. 4, No. 3, Fall, 1980, pp. 201-207.

651. "Story of Swahili, An In Language", U.S. News & World Report, Vol. 66, No. 13, March 31, 1969, p. 8.

652. Stovel, John E. "Black Studies Is White Studies", Social Studies, Vol. 62, No. 5, October, 1971, pp. 204-208.

653. "Studies in Ethnics Falling Cff", Washington Post, October 8, 1972, p. G-7.

654. Stuckey, Sterling. Black Studies and White Myths", New York Times, February 13, 1971, p. 27.

655.* _____ . "Contours of Black Studies: The Dimension of African and Afro-American Relationships", Massachusetts Review, Vol. 10, No. 4, Autumn, 1969, pp. 747-756.

656. "Summer Institute in Afro-American Studies", School Teacher, February 28, 1969.

657. Swanston, David. "How to Wreck Campus Violence at San Francisco State College", Nation, Vol. 206, No. 2, January 8, 1968, pp. 38-41.

658. "TEACHING Black Culture", Time, Vol. 91, No. 24, June 14, 1968, p. 46.

659.*Terrell, Robert L. "Black Awareness Versus Negro Traditions: Atlanta University Center", New South, Vol. 24, No. 1, 1969, pp. 29-40.

660. "Tex. U Officials Meet Student Demands For Course in Negro History", New York Times, May 8, 1969, p. 32.

661. "The Agony of Cornell (University)", Time, Vol. 93, No. 18, May 2, 1969, pp. 38-39.

662. "The Negro in History Textbooks", Crisis, Vol. 62, No. 7, August-September, 1965, pp. 427-428.

663. "The Scranton Report, The Black Student Movement", Chronicle of Education, Vol. 4, No. 2, October 5, 1970, pp. 11-14.

664.*Thelwell, Mike. "Black Studies: A Political Perspective", Massachusetts Review, Vol. 10, No. 4, Autumn, 1969, pp. 703-712.

665.* _____ . "Black Studies and White Universities", Ramparts, Vol. 7, No. 12, May, 1969.

666. Tinney, James S. "A Unit on Black Literature", English Journal, Vol. 58, No. 7, October, 1969, pp. 1028-1031.

667.*Tischler, Nancy M. "Negro Literature and Classic Form", Contemporary Literature, Vol. 10, Summer, 1969, pp. 352-355.

668. Turner, Clarence Rollo. "Some Theoretical and Conceptual Considerations For Black Family Studies", Black Lines: A Journal of Black Studies, Vol. 2, No. 4, Summer, 1972, pp. 13-27.

669. Turner, Darwin T. "The Center for African and Afro-American Studies at North Carolina Agricultural and Technical State University", Journal of Negro Education, Vol. 39, No. 3, Summer, 1970, pp. 221-229.

670. Turner, James. "Black Studies and A Black Philosophy of Education", Black Lines: A Journal of Black Studies, Vol. 1, No. 2, Winter, 1970, pp. 5-8.

671.*_____. "Black Studies and a Black Philosophy of Education", Imani, August/September, 1971, pp. 12-17.

672.*_____. "Black Studies As An Integral Tradition in African-American Intellectual History", Journal of Negro Education, Vol. 49', No. 1, Winter, 1980, pp. 52-59.

673. _____. "Student's View: Black Students and Their Changing Perspective", Ebony, Vol. 24, No. 10, August, 1969, pp. 135-140.

674. Turner, William. "A Position on the Question of Ethnical Neutrality in Social Science", Journal of Afro-American Issues, Vol. 1, No. 3, Winter/Spring, 1973, pp. 323-330.

675. "Two Societies: Voluntary Segregation on College Campuses", Times, Vol. 100, No. 22, November 27, p. 40.

676. "UNDER Federal Fire: Black Studies", U.S. News & World Report, Vol. 66, No. 11, March 17, 1969, p. 13.

677. VAN DEBURG, William L. "Afro-American Studies: A Question of Preservation", Negro History Bulletin, Vol. 37, No. 4, June/July, 1974, pp. 262-264.

678.*Vontress, Clemmont E. "Black Studies-Boon or Bane?" Journal of Negro Education, Vol. 39, No. 3, Summer, 1970, pp. 192-200.

679. WADINASI, Sedeka (Hiram Nall) "The Status of Black Studies at CSULA (California State University at Los Angeles)", Black Collegian, Vol. 7, No. 3, January/February, 1977, pp. 18-21.

680. Walden, Daniel. "Teaching Negro History, One White Experience", School and Society, Vol. 97, No. 2217, April, 1969, pp. 232-233.

681.*Walker, S. Jay. "Black Studies: Phase Two", American Scholar, Vol. 42, No. 4, Autumn, 1973, pp. 604-615.

682. *Walters, Ronald W. "Critical Issues on Black Studies", Pan-African Journal, Vol. 3, No. 3, 1970, pp. 127-139.

683. _____. "The Discipline of Black Studies", Negro Educational Review, Vol. 21, No. 4, October, 1970, pp. 138-144.

684. *Walton, Sidney F., Jr. "Black Studies and Affirmative Action", Black Scholar, Vol. 6, No. 1, September, 1974, pp. 21-31.

685. Wandamacher, Nicholas. "Afro-American Studies", Bulletin of the National Association of Secondary School Principals, Vol. 54, No. 2, 1970, pp. 43-50.

686. Wansley, J. "With the Discovery of Our Nig, Henry Gates Becomes the Sherlock Holmes of Black Studies", People's Weekly, Vol. 20, No. 1, September 12, 1983, pp. 15-16.

687. Warr, J. "Black History and Culture", NCEA Bulletin, Vol. 65, May, 1969, pp. 51-55.

688. Waugh, William J. "Black Studies Winning Strong Scholarly Support", Register-Guard (Eugene, Oregon), July 19, 1970, p. 13D.

689. Weinland, Thomas P. and Arthur D. Roberts. "In Search of Humanity", Educational Leadership, Vol. 28, No. 4, January, 1971, pp. 364-368.

690. Weinstein, A. "Passion and Pity in Black Studies", Trans-Action, Vol. 35, No. 6, June, 1971, pp. 28-29.

691. *Wells, Elmer E. "Black Studies, An Educational Dilemma", Negro History Bulletin, Vol. 36, No. 2, February, 1973, pp. 29-33.

692. Wentworth, Eric. "Maryland Department of Education Urges Black Studies in All Schools", Washington Post, February 6, 1970, p. 1.

693. Wesley, Charles H. "Black Studies and History Week", Negro History Bulletin, Vol. 35, No. 2, February, 1972, pp. 28-29.

694. *_____. "The Need For Research in the Development of Black Studies Program", Journal of Negro Education, Vol. 39, No. 3, Summer, 1970, pp. 263-273.

695. *West, Carole Cannon and Allen Williams. "Awareness: Teaching Black Literature in the Secondary School", Journal of Black Studies, Vol. 3, No. 4, June, 1973, pp. 455-471.

696. *Weston, Martin. "Black Studies: Dead or Alive?" Essence, Vol. 5, No. 4, August, 1974, pp. 56-57, 68-69.

697. "What Negro Students Demand and What They Get", U.S. News & World Report, Vol. 64, No. 23, June 24, 1968, pp. 82-84.

698. "What White Colleges Are Doing on Black Studies", Jet, Vol. 36, No. 2, February 20, 1969, p. 50.

699. "What White Students Think of Black Studies", Life, Vol. 68, No. 17, May 8, 1970, p. 34.

700. Wheeler, William B. "Teaching Negro History in the Public Schools: Let's Not Repeat Our Mistakes", Journal of Negro Education, Vol. 34, No. 1, Winter, 1970, pp. 91-95.

701.*"White Black-History Teacher Finds His Color a Handicap", Washington Sunday Star, January 4, 1970, p. A-23.

702. "White Plains, N.Y. School Pledges to Offer More Studies of Negro History and Culture in Education Curriculum", New York Times, April 7, 1969, p. 9.

703. "Why Colleges and Students Need Black Studies", NOMMO, (Purdue University) Vol. 9, No. 2, November-December, 1983, pp. 1, 11.

704.*Wilcox, Preston. "Black Studies as an Academic Discipline", Negro Digest, Vol. 19, No. 3, March, 1970, pp. 75-87.

705. Wilkins, Roger. "Black Studies: What's Left Is No Small Achievement", New York Times, March 16, 1975.

706. Williams, Kenny J. "The Black Studies Syndrome", Change, Vol. 13, No. 2, October, 1981, pp. 30-37.

707.*Williams, Louis N. and Mohamed El-Khawas. "A Philosophy of Black Education". Journal of Negro Education, Vol. 47, No. 2, Spring, 1978, pp. 177-191.

708. Williams, Ronald. "Black Studies: The Work To Come", Negro Digest, Vol. 19, No. 3, January, 1970, pp. 30-35.

709. Wilson, Charles E. "The Case for Black Studies", Educational Leadership, Vol. 27, No. 3, December, 1969, pp. 218-221.

710. Wilson, William J. "A Rejoinder To Vincent Harding", Negro Digest, Vol. 19, No. 3, March, 1970, pp. 6-11.

711.* _____. "Issues and Challenges of Black Studies", Journal of Social and Behavioral Sciences, Vol. 18, Nos. 1 & 2.

712.* _____. "The Quest For Meaningful Black Experience on White Campuses", Massachusetts Review, Vol. 10, No. 4, Autumn, 1969, pp. 737-756.

713.*Winston, Michael R. "Through The Back Door: Academic Racism and the Negro Scholar in Historical Perspective", Daedalus, Vol. 100, No. 3, 1971, pp. 678-719.

714. Wolf, Donald J. "The Dilemma of Good Men", Catholic World, Vol. 209, No. 1251, 1969, pp. 103-106.

715. Wooding, Paul. "The Struggle For Black Identity", Saturday Review, Vol. 52, No. 3, January 18, 1969, p. 62.

716.*Woodson, Carter G. "Negro Life and History in Our Schools", Journal of Negro History, Vol. 4, No. 3, July, 1919, pp. 273-280.

717. Woodward, C. Vann. "Clio With Soul", Journal of American History, Vol. 56, No. 1, June, 1969, pp. 5-20.

718. Wright, Stephen J. "Black Studies and Sound Scholarship", Phi Delta Kappan, Vol. 51, March, 1970, pp. 365-368.

719. *Wrights, Nathan, Jr. "Serving Black Students: For What?" Journal of Afro-American Issues, Vol. 1, No. 2, Fall, 1972, pp. 131-140.

720. "YALE'S New Afro-American Studies Program", School and Society, Vol. 97, No. 2317, April, 1969, pp. 206-207.

721. "Yale U to Allow Undergrads to Major in Negro Culture", New York Times, December 13, 1969, p. 43.

722. *Yee, Albert H. and Marvin J. Fruth. "Do Black Studies Make a Difference in Ghetto Children's Achievement and Attitudes", Journal of Negro Education, Vol. 42, No. 1, Winter, 1973, pp. 33-38.

723. Young, Herman A. and Barbara H. Young. "Science and Black Studies", Journal of Negro Education, Vol. 46, No. 4, Fall, 1977, pp. 380-387.

724. Young, Whitney. "Black Studies", New York Daily News, February 3, 1969.

725. ZUNINO, Gerald, J. "Afro-American History Curricula in the Senior High School", Phylon, Vol. 34, No. 1, March, 1973, pp. 78-85.

INDEX

Including authors, joint authors, and editors. Numbers refer to individual entry numbers.

About the Compilers

Lenwood G. Davis is Associate Professor of History at Winston-Salem State University. Dr. Davis has compiled more than seventy-eight bibliographies. He is the author of numerous books, the most recent of which include *Black Artists in the United States: An Annotated Bibliography*, coauthored with Janet L. Sims (1980), *Marcus Garvey: An Annotated Bibliography*, coauthored with Janet L. Sims (1980), *Black Aged in the United States* (1980), *Black Athletes in the United States: A Bibliography*, coauthored with Belinda S. Daniels (1981), *A Paul Robeson Research Guide* (1982), *Joe Louis: A Selected Bibliography* (1983), *Malcolm X: A Selected Bibliography* (1984), *The Ku Klux Klan: A Bibliography* (1984), *Black-Jewish Relations in the United States, 1752-1984: A Selected Bibliography* (1984), and *Blacks in the American Armed Forces, 1776-1983*, coauthored with George H. Hill (1984).

George H. Hill, APR, journalist, television and radio producer, and lecturer is director of the Institute of Research, vice president of Nightingale Communications & Media, and is instructor of media classes at Los Angeles Southwest College. He holds seven college degrees including a Ph.D. in communications and is accredited by the Public Relations Society of America. Dr. Hill's other books include: *Black Media in America: A Resource Guide and Bibliography*, *Airwaves to the Soul, Religious Broadcasting, 1920-1983: A Selectively Annotated Bibliography* (with Lenwood G. Davis), *Black Business and Economic Conditions: A Bibliography*, *Jessie Louis Jackson—From Country Preacher to Presidential Candidate: A Bibliography* (with Janet Sims-Wood), *Ebony Images: Black Americans & Television*, *Michael Joe Jackson: A Bio-Bibliography*, *Civil Rights Leaders and Organizations: A Bibliography*, and *Blacks in the American Armed Forced, 1776-1983* (coauthored with Lenwood G. Davis, Greenwood Press, 1984).